'Convincing people to spend hours running through the mud is no easy task. Building a business where millions of people pay money to do this would be ridiculous. But Will Dean has done it, and this gripping book reveals what it takes to stand by your values and create an organization that stands for those values'

ADAM GRANT, author of *Originals* and *Give and Take* and co-author of *Option B*

'Will Dean is one of the most important leaders of his generation – boldly pushing back on our digitally obsessed culture to get us out of our comfort zones, into the mud, working as a team and discovering all sorts of potential along the way. *It Takes a Tribe* is loaded with brilliant stories, lessons and inspiration that will make you want to jump off your couch and go make an impact!'

SARAH ROBB O'HAGAN, CEO of FlyWheel and author of *Extreme You*

IT TAKES A TRIBE

IT TAKES A TRIBE

Building the
TOUGH MUDDER
Movement

WILL DEAN

WITH TIM ADAMS

PORTFOLIO
PENGUIN

PORTFOLIO PENGUIN

UK | USA | Canada | Ireland | Australia
India | New Zealand | South Africa

Portfolio Penguin is part of the Penguin Random House group of companies
whose addresses can be found at global.penguinrandomhouse.com.

First published in the United States of America by Portfolio/Penguin,
an imprint of Penguin Random House LLC 2017
First published in Great Britain by Portfolio 2017
001

Copyright © Will Dean, 2017

Inset credits: Dmitry Gudkov, pp. 2, (bottom), 4 (bottom right), 5 (top), 5 (bottom right);
The Avielle Foundation, p. 4 (top); WENN Ltd/Alamy Stock Photo, p. 2 (middle);
Will Dean, Tough Mudder co-founder and CEO, pp. 1 (top left, top right), 2 (top);
Tough Mudder Incorporated, pp. 1 (bottom), 3, 4 (bottom left), 5 (bottom left), 6, 7, 8

The moral right of the author has been asserted

Printed in Great Britain by Clays Ltd, St Ives plc

A CIP catalogue record for this book is available from the British Library

ISBN: 978–0–241–29260–0

www.greenpenguin.co.uk

MIX
Paper from
responsible sources
FSC® C018179

Penguin Random House is committed to a
sustainable future for our business, our readers
and our planet. This book is made from Forest
Stewardship Council® certified paper.

To my parents, John and Deborah Dean

Contents

Contents

CHAPTER 1

In the Beginning:
The First Mudder

One jumps into the fray, then figures out what to do next.

– **Napoleon Bonaparte**

In May 2010, I found myself halfway up a small mountain in a deserted ski resort in Allentown, Pennsylvania, surrounded by piles of long metal poles. There was a fine rain in the air. Shouts of desperation could occasionally be heard from the pinewoods in the distance, as if from a retreating army. I was speaking to a reporter from Allentown's local paper. It was the day of the first Tough Mudder – the first day of the rest of my life – and things were not going entirely to plan.

The reporter was looking at me with some concern. I had not slept for a week, and for a couple of months had existed solely on caffeine and anxiety. A large, angry boil had erupted on one side of my face. To hide it I was scraggily unshaven and standing oddly at an angle, as if squinting around a corner, affecting what I hoped was an air of lofty British authority.

'So, Will,' the reporter said, trying to catch my eye, 'what are you doing here today in Allentown?'

This was a question that loomed large in my own thoughts. Though usually with a couple of stronger words added between 'what' and 'are'. There was a short answer and a long answer.

The short answer went something like this. 'I am trying to create seventeen obstacles – partly out of these long metal poles – on the edge of a town I know only from a Billy Joel song. These obstacles must be both dramatically risky and generally safe and spaced out over a seven-mile course up and down this mountain and through these pinewoods. Neither I nor my team of volunteers – mostly friends from England – actually have any direct experience building obstacles. Nor do we have any blueprints for them. Still, we have been doing this (with the help of the ski resort maintenance department) to the best of our ability so that several thousand people, many of them veterans of the world's most demanding endurance events, or members of the US military fresh home from war zones or officers serving in the local police and fire departments, will not shortly be chasing me up this mountain, over those obstacles, and demanding their money back.'

The longer answer was even more complicated.

I was twenty-nine years old. Two years earlier I had walked out on a fast-track career in the British Foreign Office, in which I had worked intensively for five years on classified counter-terrorist operations in the Middle East and Afghanistan. I had spent those subsequent two years and the little money I had saved acquiring an MBA at Harvard Business School, in the possibly misguided belief that by doing so I would learn how to be an entrepreneur.

Most of my peers from Harvard, who had also spent two years and all that money, were by now counting the zeros on job offers from Wall Street private equity firms. Or playing volleyball with their stock options on a campus in Silicon Valley. My own efforts in that career-orientated direction consisted of a six-week trial at the elite management consulting firm Bain & Co., mostly, if I'm honest, on my mother's long-ago insistence that I at least 'try a proper job'. My enthusiasm for suit wearing and salary drawing had become boredom by day three. Boredom that I imagined would be my primary experience, had I stayed, for the remaining thirty years of my career.

My subsequent inactivity, and its effect on my personal balance sheet, had not gone unnoticed, however.

My girlfriend, Katie, herself recently graduated from Harvard Law School and equally weighed down by debt, had generously, if pointedly, offered to support me 'for a year' if bad came to worse.

Citibank, the owner of my student loan, was proving less supportive. My 'relationship manager' had called earlier that week to ask the $100,000 question: when, and by what means, would I start making payments against their bet on my future? He gave me the helpful advice that, if I did not start now, my $100,000 question would quickly become a $150,000 one.

I had, I believed, developed habits of strategic thinking in practice in my years working in counter-terrorism and in theory in my time studying at Harvard. Still, standing halfway up that mountain, my strategizing had somehow led me to decide that the most logical next step in my life was this: I was going to create a weekend adult obstacle course, with the help of some coerced friends, at Bear Creek Ski Resort outside Allentown, Pennsylvania, in the off-season.

Neither of these answers, short or long, was what I said to the reporter.

I talked instead about my hopes for what we were billing as 'probably the toughest event on the planet', and I took a stab at describing our as yet unformed Tough Mudder tribe. 'If you are going to describe what a Tough Mudder is,' I said, 'you have to describe what they are not. They are not marathon runners or triathletes. They are not guys who wax their legs so they can save five seconds on their finishing time. There is no pretence about them or showing off. They get on with it. They don't moan. A Tough Mudder has fear but he or she overcomes it.'

I talked about how Tough Mudder had been deliberately conceived not as a race or another Iron Man or marathon but as an untimed challenge. About how the course could only be negotiated with help from friends and teammates and strangers – and that as such it tested a particular idea of achievement, based on mutual cooperation, not winner-take-all competition. And I ended by saying how, working out of a corner of borrowed office space in a half-abandoned building directly under the Brooklyn Bridge, we had hoped that five hundred people would sign up for this first event after we advertised it on Facebook but how nearly forty-five hundred people had actually done so.

As we spoke, for better or worse, many of those forty-five hundred people were making their way to Allentown. The first Mudders.

Some had already arrived the night before, camping out in tents or sleeping in cars, mostly men, some shirtless in the early morning, all pumped up, expectant. They had enthusiastically taken the Tough Mudder pledge that I had invented with my old high school friend Guy Livingstone, my co-founder, late one night a few weeks earlier. We had tried to pitch the pledge somewhere between Boy Scout's honour and Navy SEAL passing-out parade. It was as serious as it needed to be:

- I understand that Tough Mudder is not a race but a challenge.
- I put teamwork and camaraderie before my course time.
- I do not whine – kids whine.
- I help my fellow Mudders complete the course.
- I overcome all fears.

The pledge demonstrated our belief that there was a craving among people, particularly young people, not only for challenging experiences but for an authentic set of values they might sign up to and, over the course of the afternoon and beyond, believe in. To test that belief, we had installed tattoo artists at the finishing line to ink the whole pledge free of charge on the backs of those Mudders who had taken it most to heart. They were already doing brisk business.

Those forty-five hundred people, those first Mudders, were our great hope. They represented the first evidence that my belief that people would be intrigued by this event – maybe even would flock to it and love it – was not entirely insane. At the very least, they were the best answer I had found so far to the Harvard professors who had greeted my original idea, presented as a business plan in an annual competition, as 'too optimistic' and 'simplistic' and advised me to persevere at Bain & Co. 'Mr Dean, do you *really* think anyone will pay you to run through mud?'

My professors, whose lives were spent measuring and ranking their students and being measured and ranked themselves, did not get the attraction of a difficult challenge in which nobody was measured or ranked. It seemed to go against everything they held sacred. 'Who on earth wants to jump into ice baths and run through fire and wallow in mud on a Sunday afternoon just for the hell of it?' they asked.

My gut feeling, beyond the statistics and research of my Power-Point presentation, was: plenty of people. I suspected, too, that Harvard professors, while undoubtedly world-class experts in many aspects of business and human behaviour, were not the best people to judge a start-up based in part on paying to get muddy.

These days I occasionally lead seminars at business schools myself. Some students ask me, 'What qualities make an entrepreneur?' I tell them that one of the key qualities I'd discovered – and I grew up in a mining town in England, so I was raised on the subject – is the stubborn will to prove that you are right when everyone around you, and even most of the voices in your head, are explaining why you are wrong. I'd had plenty of opportunity to listen to those voices in the months preparing for the launch of Tough Mudder. One stuck in my mind and stayed there: the voice of a woman I had met one night in Connecticut when we were trying to get Tough Mudder off the ground.

It had taken us quite a long time to decide that the mountain outside Allentown was the best site for the first event. Guy and I had driven out to lots of potential venues a day or two's journey from New York City before committing to it, mainly because we didn't know what we were looking for until we found it. In January, I had gone out to a speedway track in the heart of rural Connecticut. I had a battered fifteen-year-old Volkswagen Jetta and the 'Check Engine' light had been flashing on and off all the way there. I got lost searching for a place that did not appear to be detectable by satellite. By the time I arrived, three or four hours from New York, it was getting dark.

Even in the gloom it was clear that I had not found what I was looking for. The track was a small dirt oval. The woman who owned and ran it was living nearby in a battered trailer with her grown-up son. She greeted me with gruff curiosity. I was too English and polite to turn mother and son down flat, so we went through the motions of trudging around the track with a torch in the freezing dark while I explained my plans.

After an hour of this, I began to make my excuses to leave, but the woman, who seemed to know firsthand and from long experience all the ways a business might go wrong, pulled me close to her and, leaning in, illuminated me in torchlight and said: 'Let me get this straight. You went to Harvard Business School and now you want to put on a mud fair at our speedway track in Connecticut?' She pulled me closer and said in a low whisper: 'Your parents must be extremely worried about you.'

In the three and a half hours driving back to Brooklyn in the Jetta with the 'Check Engine' light still flashing, the woman's words haunted me. They continued to come to mind at the more desperate moments – and there were plenty of those – in the weeks that followed. I had been putting about five hundred miles on the VW's odometer each day, looking at various fields, some even less promising than the speedway oval. As I was driving through the rural Connecticut dark that night I found myself recalling something I had read while at the Foreign Office. It was a report about the few elite Tornado pilots in the first Gulf War who had been shot down and ejected behind enemy lines. The pilots abruptly went from being in their miraculous all-seeing, high-tech machines, ten thousand feet above the planet, to a very different reality: on the ground, tangled in a parachute, with a handgun and no idea where they were or what to do.

It had been a little bit like that graduating from Harvard with no job. For two years, I had existed in an absurdly comfortable academic country club, with paintings on loan from the Louvre, being prepared to become a master of the universe on Wall Street. Suddenly here I was, having fallen from that great height, tangled up, and on the ground. Getting up at six in the morning to make myself sandwiches, wrapped in tinfoil, because I was sick of stopping at petrol stations where the only thing to eat was sweets. Sleeping in a fifteen-year-old Jetta because it was too far to the next grim motel. It was not a happy drive home.

My ambition of learning how to be an entrepreneur had proved frustrating at Harvard. It was an ambition that I had been driven by, and tried to resist, since I had set up my first business selling kids duffel bags at my secondary school. I'd hoped it might be fulfilled by the challenge and adventure of the Foreign Office, but it hadn't gone away. I thought that Harvard would give me the skills to take some of the risk out of starting on my own. That hope was no doubt a little naive. There were many useful and thought-provoking things that the business school did teach you – how to be a convincing management consultant for one – but the courses on creating your own business were, for me, frustrating and abstract. They attempted to make the principles of start-up into a science. It was an approach that involved very little about tinfoil-wrapped sandwiches and a lot about the right conditions to raise venture capital and to project valuations for structured equity deals. This science sometimes seemed to be the work of people who had never, and would never, start businesses of their own.

I had learned how to use game theory to shape strategy. I had absorbed ideas of lateral and vertical integration. I had considered the employment of fast-cycle capability for competitive advantage.

But if I'm honest, the principle I was testing in Allentown, Pennsylvania, was one most famously expressed by Kevin Costner in that sentimental movie about baseball, *Field of Dreams*: 'If you build it, they will come.'

No doubt there is a place for the science of start-ups. But there is also room for the fact that it is only by trying to sell something, with plenty at stake, that you discover whether you are right in thinking another person will buy it.

All start-ups in this sense are at least as much about intuition and stubbornness as analysis and judgement. I had done as much conventional work exploring the possibilities of bringing a mud-run event to the United States as I could. I visited the two closest equivalents to what I had in mind in Britain and in Germany. I worked up some credible figures about the rise of endurance events and their place in the lives of Generation Y. But, being honest, the moment that convinced me I had a great idea had occurred while competing in a triathlon in my first year at Harvard.

I had run in marathons and triathlons since undergraduate days and had always been troubled by their spirit. I disliked the inevitable – and apparently only – question that people asked you in the days after you had run: 'What was your time?' It was as if that was the only point of the twenty-six miles of shattering effort.

My eureka moment arrived a third of the way through a triathlon in Boston in 2008. I finished my swim and, as I struggled to get out of my wetsuit, I found that my zip was stuck. I asked first one, then another, then another of the competitors around me if they might spare the two seconds it would take to free it and allow me to get on my bike and continue with the race. They all looked at me as if I were a crazy Englishman, shrugged, hurried out of their own suits and onto their own bikes. Those two seconds I was asking them to sacrifice were two seconds off their own finishing time. And then it dawned on me: where on earth was the fun in doing this hard thing on your own against the clock? Surely there was another way?

Most of the rest of the business had been imagined in a similar accidental spirit. I had come up with the name Tough Mudder late one evening in a bar near Harvard Yard with a couple of old friends. I had been explaining the concept of cooperative mud runs, somewhat excitably, and had started writing potential names down on a paper napkin. I had rejected Spartan (too puritanical) and Warrior (too male). I wanted something a bit edgier. 'Badass Mudder,' I offered in my best English accent. There were blank faces around the table, a few smirks and shaken heads. And then: 'Tough Mudder.' The faces instantly brightened and there were nods. I phoned a friend and he liked it too. Armed with this detailed qualitative market research I left my beer unfinished, cycled the twenty minutes back to the room I was renting in a semi-derelict building on the other side of town, and registered the URL ToughMudder.com. The logo was developed with a similar degree of science. I doodled the silhouette of a man emerging from orange flames and had it drawn by a friend who knew his way around graphic design programs. And after that there was no going back.

I had called on Guy Livingstone in October 2009, when the idea for the business was becoming a now-or-never reality – I was full of those entrepreneur's fears that an idea that seemed so rich in possibility to me meant that others, too, would be seeing its potential. It was important that Tough Mudder not only started quickly but grew fast to colonize the market I believed existed. I was pretty certain I couldn't do all of it myself. I needed a partner I could trust. I had known Guy since before our voices broke. Fiercely bright and with high energy for getting things done, he'd felt he was short-changing himself as a corporate lawyer in London and had been casting around for a challenge. He had approached this in a characteristic-ally full-on way. When I contacted him, he said he had given up his job to learn Arabic and was living in Damascus, Syria, where he knew no one and was wondering what to do next. He didn't need much persuading to get on a plane and accept my offer to be Tough Mudder's chief operating officer.

That title made it sound a great deal grander than the reality. Tough Mudder at that point was a single desk in a warehouse in Brooklyn that we had borrowed from someone who ran a climbing magazine (the magazine was in the process of relocating). For the first few weeks sitting at that desk, Guy and I tried and failed to per-suade anyone we could think of to help finance our company. No one was interested. Undeterred, and a little desperate, we put in ten thou-sand dollars each (our respective life savings) and made the execu-tive decision of spending nearly half on Facebook advertising. The ads targeted those people we thought might be most interested in our first event: young professionals, trail runners, police officers, fire-fighters and soldiers who lived in and around Pennsylvania.

The website we created had gone online in early February. Our first call to arms went like this:

'Tough Mudder is not your average mud run or spirit-crushing road race. Tough Mudder is a seven-mile obstacle course designed by British Special Forces to test all-round toughness, strength, stamina, fitness, mental grit, and camaraderie . . . Participants will charge into battle with thousands of other Mudders – battle cries are essential . . . Participants are encouraged to leave their traditional running attire at home. Costumes, tattoos, and mullets are encouraged . . . Although there are no monetary prizes, the top 5 percent of finishers will be given free entry to the World's Toughest Mudder to be held in 2011, and will be first in line for the Dogfish Head brewery post-party that will feature live music, BBQ, and beer!'

On the first day after the site launched, Guy and I arrived early at our desk, waiting for a booking, wondering if our ad had hit any of the right people. There was not a single enquiry. Then two people signed up on the second day (we had a business!). Two more joined on the fourth. Then bookings started to gather momentum. A week later I called Guy to say, 'Pretty awesome day; we got ten people.' Then, a week after that, we were saying, 'Not a bad day: two hundred.' And the day before the price went from eighty dollars to ninety dollars, we got four hundred people in two hours. That was the day we got excited, the day that it became clear Tough Mudder was an actual thing existing outside of our own heads. Neither of us slept at all that night.

But who exactly were all these people who were signing up?

We did a bit of searching and Googling trying to work out who our first tribe members were. One group sparked our attention. A team of state troopers had seen our ad, and they wanted to run in honour of a fellow officer who had been killed in the line of duty some months earlier. The troopers had called themselves Team 8819, which was the ID number of the officer – Josh Miller – who had died. Miller, who was thirty-one, had been shot and killed during the successful rescue of a nine-year-old boy who had been snatched from his mother and kidnapped. He had left behind a wife and two children.

The knowledge that those troopers had signed up for Bear Creek sharpened the pressure to get that first event right. We had hoped that we could attract exactly that kind of Mudder who got the authentic emotion of what we were trying to create. We now had to do Team 8819 – and our other pioneer Mudders – some kind of justice.

This ambition was, in the weeks leading up to Bear Creek, easier said than done. Guy and I were working twenty-hour days but were also demonstrating that twenty hours were nowhere near enough. The weeks between the end of March, when we took the booking of our four thousandth potential Mudder, and May, when the event was booked to take place, were a blur of ad hoc planning.

In the launch of any start-up, fatigue makes minor mishaps feel like catastrophes. At every point, you feel one wrong step could derail you completely. Given the logistics of Tough Mudder, these feelings were exaggerated. One of the things, for example, that neither Guy nor I had much experience with was obtaining insurance for private events. But how hard could it be?

It became clear, after a few calls in April, that Tough Mudder was not going to be an event that was particularly straightforward to insure. Guy and I phoned brokers in Pennsylvania and then across the country with increasing desperation. Usually by the time we got to the point where we explained that we were billing this as 'probably the toughest event on the planet' and that it would involve five thousand people negotiating obstacles that we had not had a chance to test in any meaningful way, the phone call had generally ended.

We eventually turned up a company – in rural Ohio – that said it could help. By that point our pitch had become deliberately vague in its detail. The insurance broker who felt he could do something for us ran a small practice near Akron. His first question on the phone was: 'So this is like a big bar mitzvah–type party?'

'Well, sort of,' I said.

'How many people roughly?' the broker wondered. 'A hundred? Two hundred?'

'About four and a half thousand . . .'

The broker sounded a little startled. 'And it will be like bouncy castles and waterslides. Stuff like that?'

'That kind of thing,' I agreed.

We ended up paying the broker ten dollars per Mudder, which was probably his biggest-ever payday. He manfully put together some paperwork for the liability, a distinctly slippery proposition. The paperwork amounted to five pages of closely set small type. The document included a death waiver, which every Mudder solemnly signed and which quickly became part of the mythology of that first event. We reassured ourselves all would be fine, while vowing to make certain our insurance arrangements were considerably more robust at future events. If there were to be future events.

A week before the first Mudder, our list of priorities had taken on a nightmarish life of its own. We had spent a lot of time scouting the terrain at Bear Creek and coming up with ideas for the seventeen obstacles that would withstand the weight and pressure of the new Mudder tribe.

Timber and bulkier materials and tents had been delivered to Bear Creek. A lot of the rest of the gear that we had sourced in New York we were planning to drive up there, along with boxes of T-shirts and banners and posters that we had been accumulating in a huge pile in the Brooklyn office. If we were to have a chance of getting the obstacles built and the event constructed, everything needed to be on-site a week before. We had persuaded a pretty big media contingent to come along, not to mention the Mudders, so the thing had to look professional. Guy had reserved trailers from Avis for us to load the gear into, but when he showed up to get them, they couldn't locate our order and all the trailers were out. They sent Guy to another location across town, the only other one open on a Sunday evening, with the promise that all would be sorted out. It was a miserable night and Guy arrived in that office dripping wet, wiping rain from his glasses. When he got to the desk a bored-looking woman looked up at him and then spent a long time staring at her computer screen while Guy explained the urgency of our situation: the forty-five hundred Mudders, the volume of equipment, how we had to be on the road that night, and how we had made the reservation a month before. After disappearing for a while and a long gossipy conversation with her friend, the woman came back to inform Guy that contrary to what he had been told, she had no trailers or large vans either. The best she could offer was a minivan. She hoped that was what he was looking for, she said, and returned to her screen.

Guy is by no means an aggressive person. I've always known him to be mild-mannered and polite. But later, when he described to me the subsequent exchange, he did so in a tone I had not heard him use before. He sounded unnervingly like the character Michael Douglas played just before he lost it in a traffic jam and went on a rampage in *Falling Down*. Apparently, before picking up the keys to the minivan, Guy found himself leaning across the desk to the woman and heard himself saying, 'Your company has literally just fucked me up the arse.'

She looked at the rainwater – and possibly tears – dripping onto her counter. 'As I said,' she replied, 'that's the best deal we can offer you.'

Back in the office we had a different problem. We discovered that we had somehow registered the Mudders in the order that they had signed up but allocated them starting numbers in alphabetical order, so the forty-five hundred bib numbers did not match the forty-five hundred registration documents. We laid both out in piles and I set to work with a couple of our interns to re-sort them. I reckoned it would take two or maybe three hours. In our somewhat frenzied state of mind we were still working at it two days later.

So, for all these reasons, and many more, by the time I came to stand in a field at Bear Creek and talk to the local reporter from Allentown, I was not feeling quite on top of my game. My energy levels were not helped by the fact that for most of the week we had been building and testing obstacles on-site from early morning until late night. These included a Death March, which was essentially scaling up a black-run ski slope; Boa Constrictor, which involved crawling through twenty feet of claustrophobic drainage tunnels; a prototypical log-carrying challenge; and Swamp Stomp, in which you had to wade through a mud pit. Some of these challenges we had created ourselves, and some were developed in consultation with a friend, Nigel Thomas, a veteran of the British Marines and Special Forces, whom we had made our unofficial 'Head of Tough'. The challenges were designed to be both physically and mentally taxing, but they also, in keeping with the no man (or woman) left behind philosophy of elite army training, emphasized the critical importance of team-work. We tried to utilize the lake on-site as much as we could, so there were a series of aquatic tests: Underwater Tunnels, in which Mudders ducked under a roped barrel without being able to see the other side; The Ball Shrinker, which was two ropes hoisted above a freezing-cold snow pond that Mudders attempted to clamber across without dragging said balls in the lake; Greased Lightning, in which you slid a hundred feet down a steep hillside that was covered in a plastic sheet and into icy water; and, finally, Walk the Plank, which began as it sounded and ended with a long swim home.

As a visual climax to the event I was determined to re-create our logo – a man running through flames – in reality. We wanted to burn hay bales for this challenge and have Johnny Cash's 'Ring of Fire' blaring, but we were told that any bale burning would have to involve the supervision of the local Pennsylvania fire department. Regulations stipulated that we needed twelve firefighters and two fire engines, which seemed a lot, particularly as they were only offering to burn ten bales of hay. That sounded to me like it would last about twenty minutes, a fact we proved by setting a couple of bales on fire. I requested that they burn a thousand bales rather than ten. In the end, we compromised on six hundred bales at the finishing line, and as a result we got our forty-five hundred photos and videos of the first Mudders staggering or charging through fire, each image or video instantly shareable on social media.

There were other things about that first event that went better than we dared hope. Guy and I had long discussions about what to give the participants once they had crossed the line and become Mudders. Since this wasn't a race, a medal didn't seem right. A certificate wouldn't work: they were too muddy. T-shirts and caps felt a bit lame. I came up with the idea of headbands, which I thought might have just the right weekend kamikaze feel, with a bit of added retro seventies comedy.

As soon as the first Mudders arrived home – like swamp creatures – and started putting on their vivid orange headbands, it was clear they were going to be lasting symbols of the tribe. The headbands glowed out of the mud. We had worried a little that people would not want to put them on. It quickly became clear that they would not want to take them off.

We went around with a video camera at the starting line, collecting stories. Many Mudders had arrived in costume. There was a team of very convincing Avatars; another in somewhat disturbing leather shorts and bondage masks. There were some leathery trail runners and a few old college classmates on reunions or bachelor or bachelorette parties. There were also quite a few people who had picked up our suggestion of the event as a vivid personal challenge. One stuck in my mind, from a man who had severe facial paralysis and was struggling to talk. 'My name is Scott Miller. I'm forty-six, from New Jersey,' he said. 'Back in January I had a big brain surgery, hence the Bell's palsy . . . For three months since then I have been listening to doctors tell me every day what I can't do. This is my shot at telling them I'm tired of hearing that.'

We had spent a lot of time working out how to create some drama at the starting line. The image we had in mind was that scene in the movie *Braveheart* in which Mel Gibson as William Wallace looks down on the assembled forces of the British king Edward Longshanks at the Battle of Bannockburn. The Scots, face painted and outnumbered and mooning the English, charge into battle with a mix of reckless fear and unstoppable belief. We tried to create a similar hectic spectacle for each of the staggered start groups of five hundred Mudders. Music blared, a bagpiper played, the Mudders chanted a loud rendition of the Mudder pledge, and fireworks boomed as the count ticked down. We had a downhill start to that first race and Mudders literally tumbled over each other in their eagerness to get to the first obstacle. Standing below, I had a sense of what it might have felt like to be an English bowman in the fourteenth century.

After that, things were a bit more haphazard. We had established a makeshift information desk, partly manned by Katie, though information itself was in short supply. Our plans for a bag drop proved inadequate; we had a single tent in which Mudders dumped four thousand backpacks. There were some difficulties with crowd flow – particularly at Berlin Walls, where quite long queues formed as people waited to be hoisted over. The Greased Lightning slide down to the water also became clogged with participants and eventually had to be closed after people started reporting cuts and bruises as they descended.

And then there was the question of course distance. We'd had no gauge for this, and only a rudimentary map, so Guy and others estimated the length of the course through the pinewoods on foot. He reckoned it was about five miles. As the event got under way, Guy and I stood watching the first *Braveheart* Mudders disappear into those pinewoods – and emerge from them surprisingly soon afterwards. The first competitor reached the finishing line in thirty-seven minutes – which was either a new world record for seven miles up and down hills with swims and seventeen obstacles, or evidence that we were not very good at measuring. Others followed, some elated, some disappointed it was over so soon, all mud-caked and gasping for a beer, swapping stories.

We welcomed each Mudder home with a headband and an embrace full of genuine excitement and relief. We were slightly delirious with fatigue. One seasoned runner gave us an immediate C minus for organization – he was among those searching for one bag among four thousand in the tent where we'd stored them – but was talking in high excitement about the idea of working in a team to get around. Several more people took up the offer of free pledge tattoos and pestered Katie at the information desk about where the next event would be and how they could sign up. I was making mental notes about a few things. One was that we needed to improve our protocols for managing the sponsored Dogfish Head beer truck that we had organized along with a live band at the finishing line.

The plan was for one free beer per Mudder, but our beer-rationing system also proved to be a work in progress. It was a hot day, and the combination of sun and mud and water appeared to have had a liberating effect on inhibitions. As the afternoon went on it was clear that many of our first Mudders were absolutely wasted. Quite a few were getting naked in our fire hose showers and rolling in the mud some more. It was all very spring break.

While this party was still in full swing, Guy called me to one side to flag a potential issue. We were dismantling the course in the gloom and salvaging what could be salvaged for future events. Much of this muddy gear was piled in the field beyond the beer truck. But a question had formed in Guy's mind: what were we going to do with it all? We had spent so long thinking about making the event take place that we had given no thought to what would happen after it had finished. Not only did we have no Avis trucks but we also had nowhere to keep all our equipment until the next event, provisionally booked in California. We must have assumed we would be run out of town and there would be no next event.

We stood looking at this huge pile of muddy equipment in the middle of the field, while I called some storage facilities nearby. Most seemed to cater for domestic storage only and had a strict non-commercial policy. In the end, we crammed as much stuff as we could into the minivan and the Jetta and set off for the nearest one. The Jetta's engine warning light was still flashing, and its suspension was scraping the road all the way there.

When we arrived at this storage depot it was getting dark. The depot manager took one look at us and shook his head.

'It's home storage only,' he said. 'No business or commercial, just domestic.' He pointed at a sign.

I took the manager's arm. 'It is domestic,' I said. And then I heard myself inventing some story about how my wife and I – I pointed to one of our alarmed-looking interns standing nearby – were doing a makeover of our new apartment and had cleared this junk out. I said all of this for some reason in a poor American accent.

The manager looked at me. And he looked at my 'wife'. And we both looked at the large number of cast-iron metal poles sticking out of the back windows of my Jetta. And then, with a look that said he had seen everything, he waved us through to unpack all our worldly goods.

The following day, after the first good night's sleep we'd had in about a month, Guy and I arrived in the office around lunchtime. Oddly, one of the first calls I took that afternoon was from my 'relationship manager' at Citibank, asking if I had worked out how to pay off my student loan.

I explained to him that I would be transferring the entire amount due by the end of the day.

MUDDER SOLIDARITY: Team 8819

Seven years ago, at around the time of that first Allentown event, Guy and I wrote down a mission statement for our new business. It read, 'Grow Mudder nation into a global tribe that lives the values of courage, personal accomplishment, teamwork, and fun.' We used the words 'nation' and 'tribe' on purpose, because we had the idea that our obstacle event would be a means of creating lasting bonds between our Mudders, forged in the belief that they had been through something challenging, an adventure, a rite of passage, and survived to tell the tale. Tribes share a set of ideas about the world and a means of communicating them; the values cut across geography and gender, class and culture. We believed that the gritty nature of the challenge would emphasize those values we had identified. And that the tribe would gather around them to take on a life of its own.

Seven years later, our collective Mudder nation has surpassed all those original ambitions. In those years, more than 2.5 million people across five continents have signed up and run the twelve-mile course, overcoming the challenge. That these Mudders have become a movement and a tribe and not just an anonymous customer base can be demonstrated in many ways, but the measure I enjoy most is this one: three thousand of those Mudders wear our tattooed logo; hundreds more have the entire Mudder pledge inked on their skin.

Beyond that, if I am proudest of anything about the last seven years, it is probably this: in a world where many of us spend most of our days staring at our computer screens, half engaged, we have drawn people together in the real world, got them muddy and given them a sense of shared achievement. If nothing else, Tough Mudder is a better answer than most to that perennial Monday-morning question: 'Did you do anything interesting at the week-end?' It has acted as a factory for storytelling. There have been many Tough Mudder love affairs and countless new friendships, several marriages and a few Mudder babies. There have been stories of genuine hardship overcome, as well as innumerable tales of everyday courage and commitment and fun. These stories have been both our currency and our inspiration. This book will, between its main chapters, highlight just a few of those stories that have meant the most to us and the lessons we have learned from them.

Mudder stories and legends began to form at that very first event. Team 8819 turned up to run in honour of their fallen friend, state trooper Josh Miller, killed while thwarting a kidnapping. The team has run each subsequent year in memory both of Miller and other colleagues who lost their lives in the line of duty, each time carrying around the Tough Mudder course a vivid crimson flag bearing the number 8819, Miller's badge number. Their story, and the emotions that attended it, became a blueprint for many others.

It was a story that began, like most stories, by chance. Team 8819 signed up originally after one of the troopers, John Edwardes, happened to see our original ad – 'Tough Mudder is not your average mud run or spirit-crushing road race . . .' – pop up on his Facebook page not long after we had launched it in February 2010. Josh Miller and John Edwardes had been close friends and colleagues, and

Edwardes and his fellow troopers had been talking only that morning about doing something special to mark the first anniversary of Miller's tragic murder, which would fall in July. When Edwardes first saw the Tough Mudder ad, Josh and the anniversary instantly sprang to mind. He sent the ad around the rest of Miller's friends in the force and wondered what they thought of signing up. One of the troopers who received that note was Corporal Lou Gerber. 'When we first started talking about it, most of us took one look at Tough Mudder and all the pictures on the web page and said, "Nah, that just looks too crazy,"' Gerber recalls. 'We had no idea what it was. And then someone said: "I bet Josh would do it anyway." And we were all like: "Oh God. Okay, you're right, he would." So it was decided we should do it too.'

Like us, Team 8819 had little idea what to expect of that first Tough Mudder. The troopers were mostly in good shape; a few were ex-marines, like Miller himself had been. But still they approached the event, Gerber recalls, with proper trepidation. In the few weeks after sign-up they went into the woods and mountains after work near their station in Pennsylvania and tried to train together, practising grips and crawls and climbs. The more they trained and thought about the seven miles, the more Gerber and one or two others didn't think they were ready for it. 'At one point,' Gerber recalls, 'I remember we were incredibly doubtful about the idea; we weren't sure we could go through with it. And one of the group, my friend Tommy, said, "I think together we can." That became our motto both that year and in the years that followed.'

Of the Bear Creek event itself, Gerber recalls most vividly the vertiginous steepness of the run up the black ski slope: 'A number of people were losing their lunch at the top of that one.' If there was a disappointment, though, it was in the dubious course length and the sense that 'the finish seemed to come a bit too soon'.

The second year was a different story. The course was now twelve miles long, again at Bear Creek, but whereas in the first year it had been unseasonably warm, this time around it was very cold. There was ice and snow on the ground. When Team 8819 got to the marker that said 'seven more miles', Gerber and the rest of the team thought there was no way they could go on. But Josh Miller's widow, Angie, and their two children were there cheering them on, and they found some reserves of strength. 'Together we can!' someone yelled, and so it proved.

Three years later, 120 troopers were running Tough Mudder under Team 8819's flag in what had become an emotional annual tribute – they made a weekend of it – and a demonstration of all that they had been through together. 'Josh was a good friend and a great cop,' Gerber says. 'But more than that, there are certain people in life who make you want to be a better person. They hold themselves to such a standard that you want to raise your own standard just because you are around them. Josh was one of those guys. As the old saying goes, "A rising tide lifts all boats," and that was Josh. Tough Mudder was a way of keeping that spirit and those stories alive.'

CHAPTER 2
What Makes a Tough Mudder: Building Character

Character cannot be developed in ease and quiet. Only through experience of trial and suffering can the soul be strengthened, ambition inspired, and success achieved.

— Helen Keller

As our society becomes more risk-averse, we are often encouraged to shy away from doing things that challenge us, to avoid stresses and difficulty. We are kept close to home as children, and as adults we are fed constant messages on all our various media about the ever-changing range of threats to our security and our health. Our technology invites us to be passive consumers of experience rather than passionate creators of it. We are seduced into living life, literally, at arm's length, on our phones. I think there are serious repercussions to those habits and that they affect our happiness and health and our sense of personal growth.

If my experience in counter-terrorism prior to Tough Mudder taught me anything, it was that only when we take risks and face up directly to challenges do we learn to build confidence and resourcefulness. Tough Mudder was designed to dramatize that state of mind and offer the kind of challenges that life in the office and in front of a screen gives us all too infrequently. It was created to demonstrate that even when we are exhausted and cold and wanting to give up, we have it in us to keep going and to push others to do so, too, and that we can take real strength and enormous pleasure from that knowledge. I am proud that people often write to us after an event and say, 'My boss was bullying me at work, and I went in the day after I ran your event and said, "You don't get to speak to me like that," because I had achieved this thing for myself. Because I am a Tough Mudder.'

In her book *Grit*, social psychologist Angela Duckworth identifies the single quality that most marks out those who succeed in life, those who feel fulfilled, from those who find life one long series of frustrations. The quality boils down to this: the understanding that your personality and character are not fixed but can be shaped and strengthened by overcoming difficult experiences. There are voices in everyone's head that resist that fact, that tell us we will never achieve this or that, so there is no point in even trying. Again, our business was designed to help silence a few of those voices. One of the questions we asked ourselves when we created Tough Mudder was this: how do you create a culture and an authentic experience that will reliably deliver grit, a quality that people seem to crave but don't know how to find?

This craving, our grit-shaped hole, feels like a recent phenomenon. It is a by-product perhaps of our fortune in living, in the Western world at least, in largely peaceful times, when work is more likely to involve generating a PowerPoint presentation than any kind of hard labour. When – to put it in blunt evolutionary terms – millennia of hunting and gathering have been replaced by a trip to the supermarket. Ease and convenience are great in their way, but for many of us life no longer routinely presents the kind of challenges that once developed resilience – and genetically, psychologically, I believe we miss those challenges. In most other times and places those trials came hard and fast, and though we might not always have welcomed them, they allowed us to show what we were capable of, gave us a sense of purpose in ourselves, and a sense of belonging in our community.

I grew up in one of those places. Worksop is a mining town in the northern English Midlands, the kind of town that the British still like to call 'gritty'. They mean by this that it has plenty of rough edges, a lot of reality. To the south of Worksop is Sherwood Forest, where Robin Hood and his Merry Men tried their outlaw experiment in the redistribution of wealth – and where as a kid I was allowed to ride my bike on ancient paths through the ancient forest, in search of the kind of adventure that I read about in my favourite Just William books.

Worksop had come of age during the Industrial Revolution. Its economy was based on the surrounding coal mines and mining villages. It was made by hard-working, no bullshit people, who enjoyed a night out on payday, and who would generally do their best to help each other out in hard times. They were all in it together. When I was only three years old, however, certainly before I can properly remember, the town experienced a kind of shock to its identity from which it has never fully recovered.

The 1984 miners' strike marked the end of that gritty idea of Britain. Margaret Thatcher, in her vision of a modern service-based economy, had made it her mission to dismantle the power of the coal mining trade unions that were symbolic of the industrial past and which, in the previous decade, had threatened to bring Britain to a standstill as they defended pay and conditions against global competition. The battlegrounds, literally, were the coalfields of Yorkshire and of Nottinghamshire. Worksop, where I lived, was on the border between the two.

For some months in 1984 the striking workers of Yorkshire and Nottinghamshire looked likely to stand together against Mrs Thatcher. The government, however, using a strategy of divide and conquer, suggested that its plan was not to close all coal mining but only the most struggling pits. Most of those pits were in Yorkshire. As the hardships of the strike continued, many Nottinghamshire miners – including those in the profitable pits around Worksop – crossed picket lines. Neighbours and families were bitterly divided by the strikebreakers' action. That loss of unity meant the Yorkshire miners' battle was doomed. Mrs Thatcher's government subsequently went back on its promise to keep profitable mines open, and the economy of Worksop, and many towns like it, collapsed along with any sense of shared purpose.

Though this conflict did not involve my family directly – my dad was a partner in a small solicitor's office above a shop in Worksop High Street – it cast a shadow over the place itself during my childhood years. It was the kind of shadow familiar to post-industrial towns across the Western world. There was the immediate issue of unemployment, but also the lasting scars of strikebreaking and betrayal. The close community of the town was fractured. Drug addiction became a major problem. By the year 2000, one in three households in Worksop had a heroin user.

I don't know how conscious I was of all that while I lived in

Worksop, but I remained affected enough by it that when I later went away to Bristol University to study economics, I returned to the town to try to answer a nagging question. I was interested in using economic theory to see if I could explain the rival motivations of the miners: the desire to stick together, apparently against many of their individual better interests, or the decision to return to work in a desperate effort to look after themselves. The nature of that stubbornness, and the consequences of its loss, fascinated me.

I came across that dissertation recently. It used ideas like the 'bandwagon effect' to describe behaviour. In all cases, it seemed the miners acted to maximize self-interest, but crucially that self-interest was not always financial, as my economic models predicted; the ties that bound the miners and their families were just as likely bonds of solidarity and shared cultural values.

That thought, and the sense that nothing had come along to properly replace those values, stayed with me.

I spoke to several men about their memories of the strike. One miner suggested 'men just wanted to get involved. The sense of loyalty to other miners was unbelievable.' Others suggested that the resistance to strikebreaking was the result of weighing the long-term consequences of crossing a picket line: 'No one would ever speak to them again, no one would drink with them, their wives would be ostracized, and nobody's children would play with theirs.' Belonging mattered, almost above all else, and was policed accordingly.

That idea of belonging, in the Worksop of my teens – and across the post-industrial landscape of the Western world – was already just a kind of memory. Its absence resulted in a loss of identity. In the past in working towns, grit – the product of hardships shared and overcome – had been something under the skin, something ingrained. It was one of the qualities that held people together. Now it was something that people were nostalgic for.

I tell this story here to begin to offer an answer to the question posed by the title of this chapter: What Makes a Tough Mudder? It's my belief that ideas for new businesses that capture people's imagination don't ever arise by accident. There is a kind of inevitability about them. They form as answers to questions that have existed in their founders' minds for years before finding the right expression. To a degree these things are subconscious. But I'm sure it wasn't entirely by chance that having grown up in a place that had dramatically lost its identity and purpose, I was drawn to try to create a business and a culture that might offer a version of those values in a different way and to a new generation.

Did I already carry some of that nostalgia for grit and camaraderie with me from Worksop when my parents made a huge financial sacrifice and sent me away to an exclusive boarding school at age thirteen? I'd like to think so. The result of that sacrifice was not necessarily the one my parents thought they were paying for, though. I felt that I didn't quite belong in the rough-edged town of my birth, but I also wasn't convinced I belonged in the more privileged world of the English shires a hundred miles south. A place where nobody but me seemed to come from an industrial town at all. I went from one community that I didn't fit into to another – but again, as something of an outsider, there were aspects of that new culture that intrigued me, that got me thinking about how shared values might be created, how I might feel like I belonged.

English boarding schools, prior to Harry Potter, were imagined primarily as factories not of wizardry but of leadership. In the nineteenth century, they were made to produce the men who would run the empire. If working towns generated one kind of grit, boarding schools were designed to create an elitist version of that same quality. They called it 'character'. Though the environment was very different, the principles – of formative experiences involving hardship and rigour, experiences overcome in part through a sense of loyalty and community – were comparable. The first headmaster of Stowe School, a very similar institution to Oundle, where I went, famously observed that his goal was to produce generations of young men who 'felt acceptable at a dance and invaluable in a shipwreck'. 'Character' was about being prepared for any crisis and being at home in any social situation. Traces of those ideas remained at Oundle, but mostly in a series of rules and traditions in which I had not much interest at all.

The whole of my first year there was spent trying to tell my parents I didn't want to be at this kind of school, calling them up in tears. Realizing I couldn't change their mind, I developed another strategy. I figured out pretty quickly that as I wasn't considered one of the really smart kids, and I didn't have an older brother, and I wasn't from a wealthy family, the only way for me to survive was to play rugby. I wasn't very skilful, but I was big and strong and would tackle anyone and run all day long. Off the rugby pitch I was like an in-betweener in the TV series. I wasn't a smoker and I wasn't a geek. It was quite a violent school, lots of fights, but I made sure I only ever had one. Told that another kid was preparing to beat me up, I squared up to him and hit him twice, hard, which unfortunately broke his front teeth. But I was never challenged again.

If I were to be asked the questions, what did you learn at school? What did you take away from that 'character factory' that led to you creating Tough Mudder? I could, like anyone, give you a list of exam grades or the odd prize. I could tell you about friendships, some of them lasting, including with my eventual Tough Mudder co-founder, Guy Livingstone. But I believe the things that make us who we are, that create one's character, give us some grit, are often accidental or surprising, noticed by us and no one else.

In this sense, looking back now, I value just three experiences out of the five years at Oundle. The first was one of those small life lessons that changed me for ever. At fourteen I had been at Oundle for nearly a year when one afternoon, a prefect, four years older than I, stopped me in the corridor and said the ten words that represented my worst nightmare: 'Dean, we need you on the house debate team tonight.'

Terror in a single sentence. I had spent most of that year as the new boy in a very traditional school trying to do or say nothing that drew attention or marked me out. I pleaded with the prefect. 'I actually can't get up and talk in front of everyone,' I said, desperately. Better excuses refused to come. 'I just can't do it.'

'Dean, you're doing it. There's no one else.'

It is hard to explain now the sense of dread that I felt the rest of that day. The debate was in the school's old hall, and nearly all the thousand or so boys would be there in the hope that someone might dry up or die on their feet and create that night's entertainment. The topic of the debate was a motion opposing gun control. I was to speak against the motion.

When the time came – seven thirty exactly, I can still remember watching the clock – I walked out on the stage in front of the rows of expectant faces, clutching my hopeless notes, preparing for humiliation. I stood for a moment paralysed. And then I remember starting to speak.

I have done a lot of public speaking since then and have learned to love it. But if you had told me it was something I would become capable of enjoying as I walked out onto that stage, at age fourteen, I wouldn't have believed it possible. The moment of revelation came when suddenly, strangely, I heard coherent words and sentences come out of my mouth and start to fill the hall. I could see the faces that had been ready to laugh start to listen. I'm not going to claim the speech was a profound addition to the gun lobby argument, but it got a few laughs and a solid round of applause. And I walked off that stage and woke up the next morning feeling different, a bit bolder, changed.

There was nothing at all exceptional in that experience, of course. Facing an audience is something nearly everyone has had to do at one time or another. But still, in those few minutes on stage I'd taken to heart a lesson that I've tried hard to live by ever since and which was central to the creation of Tough Mudder: I had done something that was truly petrifying to me, and I had come through. I felt better as a result. I had learned one of life's simple, crucial lessons: that by doing genuinely challenging things I could change the way I thought of myself and how others thought of me.

The second lesson I learned at school came from a maths teacher, who saw something in me, singled me out for praise, moved me up to the top set, and once told my parents that in all his years of teaching he had only once or twice come across a boy as bright as me. This news came at the time as a total shock both to me and to them. It brought to mind that provocative research that suggests the key difference between success and failure in life is often down to a very simple fact: those people who are told that they have what it takes to succeed often do. Those who are not, more often don't. As with the experience of standing in the hall debating, I took that teacher's words to heart. He said I could do something special or different. I set my mind on proving him right.

The last experience that stayed with me was an incident that happened in my final year at Oundle. The school was organized on a boarding-house system. In my prefect year, the boys in my house thought it was cool to be arrogant and rude as a group to the house-keepers. The cleaners were mocked as 'skivs'. Boys would say, 'Who cares if we make a mess? The skivs are going to skiv it up.' At the end of one term the cleaners complained about this rudeness and all the boys in the house were called in front of the matron, who looked after us. We stood there and she read a letter from the cleaners. It contained this line: 'The only boy who treats us with any respect is William Dean, and we think he gets in trouble from the others for being kind to us.' The matron expanded on this: 'William Dean is the only one that has got the balls to show any manners.'

That one sentence is perhaps the thing I am most proud of from all my time at school. Most of the cleaners in our boarding-house were women from poor backgrounds who were working to supple-ment incomes. It wasn't like I was the only kid there who understood that and what it meant. But there was a very strong peer pressure to be a snobby little shit, which I refused to join in with. I did get some stick for it. More after the matron had singled me out. 'Why are you so fucking gay, Dean?' was a favourite line. But I didn't care that much. I talk now sometimes to the Tough Mudder team about setting our own standards, about not doing the easy thing, but always trying to do the right thing. And when I do, sometimes that grim word 'skivs' comes to mind.

That doesn't seem like very much to take away from five years of expensive education, but I think those few lessons gave me some understanding that 'character building' is exactly what the phrase suggests: one formative brick of a challenging experience, however small, laid on top of another. One obstacle overcome, and then the next. The important thing, it seems to me, is to find a culture in which you are encouraged to go out and look for those experiences, to see what you might be capable of.

I left Oundle with that thought firmly in mind. In my gap year between boarding school and university, rather than heading for the beaches of Australia with some friends to drink too much beer (tempting though that was), I worked for several months at a London tabloid, in a culture fuelled by cynicism and cocaine, before taking myself off to travel alone in Pakistan for half a year. (I still have a photograph in which I am drinking tea outside the Osama bin Laden Barbers in Peshawar, a name that meant nothing to me then.)

It intrigues me now to think that I decided to travel in those places alone. I was happy enough in the role of outsider, but I think I was still above all restless for a sense of belonging, a place where I truly felt I fitted in. University didn't quite satisfy that restlessness – it seemed like a means to an end – but I had high hopes of discovering that elusive feeling when I subsequently joined the British Foreign Service. I put in five challenging years working in counter-terrorism – a role I took on soon after 9/11, when the Western world's governments and intelligence agencies were desperately trying to catch up with the new global realities. In order to enter that service, I passed through a training programme that tested, in particular, my psychological reserves for six intense months. I felt that I had gone into it primed for failure. Ten potential recruits are hand chosen for the elite training each year. Nine make it through. As by far the youngest and least experienced candidate – I was a twenty-three-year-old economics graduate up against hardened army officers and high-flying individuals with five or six years of corporate experience – I appeared destined to be the odd one out. That conviction was cemented when on the way down to my first day of training, my car was rear-ended at a junction and I got severe whiplash. In a desperate effort to overcome the discomfort, and make it through my first day, I seriously overdid the painkillers the hospital gave me. I reported for duty in what my fellow trainees subsequently described as 'a state of stumbling catatonia'. The weird first impression I made on the training instructor appeared, in their eyes, and his, to have sealed my fate.

The specifics of the training are confidential, but they had evolved in the Foreign Service in the years since the Second World War to test every aspect of your determination, ingenuity and courage under extreme pressure. Some of the training took place in Britain, some on assignment in more alien locations. Over the course of those months, despite that distinctly shaky start, I demonstrated enough of the required qualities to make sure that in the end I was not the recruit who was dropped. I then set about utilizing all that I had learned in that training, often working alone in the Middle East, tasked with creating strategies that would reveal and undermine the organization of terrorist cells.

In many ways, I found in both the challenge and camaraderie of that work the sense of purpose and belonging I had been restless for growing up. I wouldn't say it made me fearless, but it gave me a belief that there were few things in life I couldn't take on. I worked alongside some genuinely inspiring people who put service before personal glory. That service also, as you can imagine, came complete with lots of rules and regulations. In fact, probably way more rules and regulations than you can imagine. A few of those rules and regulations saved people's lives. Many of them were a pain in the arse.

The Foreign Service was making noises about how, to counter the new reality of the world, it would have to be far more entrepreneurial, innovative and flexible, which was one of the reasons I was attracted to it, and it to me. I think perhaps partly because I had never felt as though I fit into the cultures of my formative years, I had developed a very strong sense of self-reliance. I had my own ideas of how things might be done most effectively and tried to live up to standards I set for myself. Some of this made me effective in that environment. Some was viewed suspiciously. To achieve anything, you had to work around the system, and though I felt I was quite good at that, there came a point when I felt a bit suffocated by the effort. It was a hard job to leave, but when I looked around at those men and women who stayed, whose optimism had been sometimes defeated by frustration, I knew I owed it to myself to get out and at least try something different.

By this point I had developed a conviction in my mind that the surest way to find the experiences I was looking for would be by trying to create and lead a business and a culture of my own. I took my search for a sense of challenge and belonging, those two crucial components of a fulfilled life, to Harvard. I went there once again with the kind of expectations that could never honestly be satisfied. There are, as I quickly discovered, few places on earth that talk more engagingly about the value of teamwork and show less interest in it in practice. Harvard selects the most competitive individuals from five continents and requires them to compete for two years. To some degree, I was no different.

I believe we all are driven to a greater or lesser extent by the need to overturn limiting ideas of ourselves, to find opportunities to show what we are made of. Often, it is comparatively minor slights that give these feelings their sharpest edge. If I'm honest, it was probably one of those slights that led me to Harvard. At eighteen my application for a place at Oxford University was unsuccessful. There is still, in Britain, an unwritten belief to do with class and tradition (there are many unwritten beliefs to do with class and tradition) that the only university degrees that count come from Oxford or Cambridge. That's clearly not true, but it is a perception I've lived with – at the Foreign Office in particular, where I was the only so-called redbrick graduate accepted on the elite programme – for all my adult life. 'You must have done really well at Bristol to get here' is a phrase I became very tired of hearing.

This shouldn't have mattered to me, intellectually or socially. Having spent several years enduring the regimented life of boarding school, I was never enthralled by the idea of further education. I only applied to Bristol at the last minute after six months away travelling in Southeast Asia; still, I had thrived in my time there in a way I may not have done at Oxford. Despite all that, I'd never forgotten the sadness (and the efforts to hide that sadness) on my parents' faces when I opened the letter saying I had been rejected by Oxford. They sacrificed a great deal for me and Oxford was the unspoken goal of that sacrifice. No one wants to feel that they have let their parents down, or not lived up to their own ambitions. The memory of that look of sadness was a big reason for me subsequently applying to Harvard – 'I'll show them' – and it was justified in one sense, in that when I was offered a place there, it was the only time I saw my dad cry with pride. If I'm honest with myself now, though, I can also see that going to an Ivy League college was a kind of vanity on my part – an expensive way of proving to myself what deep down I already knew: that most people at elite universities aren't touched by genius or brilliance but are, generally, privileged, lucky, conscientious and competitive. I ended up doing fine in this company, finishing as an honours student in the top 15 per cent of my year. I also made some good and lasting friendships and was often inspired by the insights of my teachers. But I was no doubt hopelessly naive to go to Harvard looking for a sense of real belonging. My naivety didn't last much beyond the first day.

On the first morning, a professor gave us a talk about what a wonderful free-thinking opportunity we had committed ourselves to and how we now belonged to a culture of enquiry like no other. Then we went around the room introducing ourselves.

The first three people happened to be three young women sitting together. And they all said, one after the other, 'I've been working in finance in New York and I have a boyfriend in New York who also works in finance.' It was the first day, and so everyone was a little bit nervous. By the time the third girl gave the same reply, it became a bit of a joke.

The fourth introduction came from a guy sitting next to them. In an attempt to continue the joke, he said, 'I also worked in finance in New York and I, of course, also have a boyfriend in finance in New York.' There were a few laughs, we carried on, and I didn't think anything more of it.

But the next day, before our first lecture, this same guy, the fourth guy in line, was standing on stage facing us. He was clearly there under duress. Unlike the day before, he was ashen and trembling a little. He went into an elaborate prepared apology about how he was ashamed of the previous day's homophobic comments. He felt he had not only let himself down but also the institution of Harvard Business School. A professor followed these comments by declaring that Harvard was a 'safe space' and homophobia would not be tolerated. The guy next to me, who became a friend, leaned across and whispered, 'Is this a show trial?' It certainly looked like one. Looking around the room, I could see everyone thinking the same thing: 'Forget about freedom and enquiry. I need to be pretty damn careful about what I say here because this poor guy is going to spend the two years being something of an outcast.'

One of the things people seemed to really invest time and intellectual energy in at Harvard was finding new reasons to be offended or outraged. This created a curious climate. There were serious arguments about how students should be banned from disrupting seminars by going to the toilet, because time was money. Someone had worked out a cost analysis of how a general lack of foresight in bladder control was depriving him of so many dollars' worth of teaching time.

No behaviour went unscrutinized. Seminars lasted eighty minutes, with the last fifteen minutes of each seminar devoted to recapping what had gone before. In certain classes, such as finance, that was incredibly helpful to me because I was generally wondering what the bloody hell had been going on for the last hour. In other classes, though, I thought I had understood what was going on for the last hour. Sometimes in those classes I was in the habit of using those final fifteen minutes to read something unrelated to the class. It turned out some people were offended by this behaviour. A woman behind me took a series of iPhone photographs of me reading from the wrong book so she could report me for not paying full attention in class. I was duly summoned to explain myself.

These kinds of behaviours were the direct product, it seemed to me, of a system that worked by never giving students objective marks or scores but instead ranking them against each other. Everyone at Harvard (with the possible exception of me) had got there by always being at the top of their class. The possibility of being near the bottom of a group and to be judged accordingly seemed to terrify people. Worse, there was never an explanation of how the rankings were decided, which was at least good preparation for a corporate culture in which being in the lowest 10 or 20 per cent of bottom line performers meant dismissal, regardless of your 'real' effort and contribution. This attitude was clearly corrosive. It set against each other very able people who might have achieved far more through collaboration. What kind of preparation was that for life?

Outside of class, people found other arenas in which to compete. We were on average about twenty-eight years old, so the desperation to be cool hadn't entirely disappeared. There were a lot of great individual people at Harvard, some of whom are still my close friends, but few of them were cool by the traditional metrics of what it meant to be cool – rebellion, creativity and attitude. We were mostly nerds doing spreadsheets. We were, to my constant English surprise, students who as a matter of course applauded our lecturers at the end of every single lecture, good or bad, without question. I had hoped after the rule-bound intensity of the Foreign Office that there would be a kind of accepting, just-be-yourself spirit to college life. In fact, the peer pressure around things like drinking a lot was worse than at boarding school. I was in my late twenties by this point. I was often thinking, *I don't want to have five beers in the first fifteen minutes of getting to this bar because frankly I am a bit of an idiot when I have had five beers*. At graduation, I received the 'too cool for school award' because I didn't go to enough class parties or something.

I don't think Harvard culture was at all unique in any of these attitudes, but it did seem to me an extreme case of some of them. There was rarely any sense of doing anything at all just for the hell of it. Time was precious. Having spent the five years before Harvard in an environment where seriousness was appropriate, and laziness or bad decision making could cost lives, I found this artificial intensity hard to take. In his account of life at HBS, *What They Teach You at Harvard Business School*, Philip Delves Broughton described students as 'insecure overachievers'. His report that a large percentage of Harvard MBAs end up being treated for depression both while there and in later life didn't surprise me. The expectations are so great, the competition so fierce, and the fear of failure so crippling. Happiness becomes another thing to rank yourself by; and there is always someone happier than you.

No doubt I was there at a particularly weird moment in the life of the institution. I started at the end of 2007, the last year of the boom in financial markets, which had gone on so long it seemed like it might go on for ever. In retrospect, it felt like the end of an era. When Lehman Brothers crashed, we MBAs were invited by one professor to observe a minute's silence. I've no doubt that kind of sentiment has changed dramatically in light of events, and the scrutiny of behaviours that caused those events, but that was all to come. At the time, there was a very clear social pecking order, based entirely on the two metrics that grads – and, apparently, the wider society – then cared about the most: how much money you were making before you arrived and how much you would be making when you left. By that measure, the people who had worked in private equity were always at the top. There was an implied assumption that if you were smart, you wanted to make a lot of money, and private equity was probably the best guarantee of doing that.

I went through Harvard with two perceived disadvantages, which made me seem crazy or dumb, among my peers if not among my professors. The first was that not only had I not worked in private equity, I had, almost uniquely, worked 'in government'. The general assumption, based on measuring success by salary, was I had done that because I couldn't find anything better to do. The other thing that marked me out as weird was this: I had declared that I was not at Harvard to learn how best to take risks with other people's money, but that I wanted to learn how to take risks with money of my own. Money that, admittedly, I did not have.

If this desire to be an entrepreneur, to start a business, at the time marked me as eccentric – why take risks when you could walk into a job with just rewards? – some of the things I said in lectures apparently made me seem like a real extremist. I was in the habit of arguing – partly on the basis of lessons I had learned growing up in Worksop and, afterwards, in the Foreign Service – that sometimes people are motivated by things other than financial gain. That sometimes they make choices that have nothing to do with price but everything to do with value. That success in life – and happiness – could not be measured only in bottom lines. As soon as I started to say any of these things I could see my fellow students raising their eyebrows, smirking: 'There goes the Marxist Will on his left-wing rants.' If I learned one thing in those seminars, it was a desire to prove those people wrong, to show that there were plenty of things that money could not always buy: community, fun, friendship and belonging. Tough Mudder was in part my effort to demonstrate that fact.

Before I got to that particular demonstration, I stumbled on the oldest proof that the very best decisions in life rarely came about through judicious planning. They happened when you made yourself a bit vulnerable and took a risk. My great abiding luck at Harvard was to meet my wife, Katie, though it seemed less like chance than fate. I was getting towards the end of my studies for my MBA and living with my friend Matt on the margin of the business school society in a house on an otherwise abandoned block half an hour from the campus. One evening we had been invited to a pretentious après-ski-themed party. We'd had a couple of beers and decided to go as pirates – because, why not? We made ridiculous costumes and swords out of tinfoil. Bicycling on the way there, Matt said he needed to stop by this other party to see a friend on his Russian course. When we got to the apartment where his friend was, Matt had to take a phone call and motioned me on up ahead because it was freezing cold outside. I assumed it was a house party. In fact, it was six Harvard law students quite stiffly having dinner. I walked in the door unannounced in my pirate costume holding a tinfoil sword.

Katie was one of the people sitting at the table, staring at me in alarm. She was talking to a guy next to her. Because I was a bit drunk, or dressed as a pirate, or to break the ice, I found myself saying: 'You're a couple?' and Katie and the guy both shook their heads nervously. By now, everyone at the table was staring at the English pirate, so I said, quite out of character, brandishing my tinfoil sword, 'If this guy is not your boyfriend, who is your boyfriend?' Katie said quietly: 'I haven't got a boyfriend.'

'Oh,' I said, piratically, 'in that case I'll get your number.' This exchange confirmed the very worst ideas that everyone around the table had about the outsize ego of Harvard MBA students. Katie took me to the kitchen. I braced myself for a lecture about rudeness and sexism and how dare I? Instead, she said, 'Here's my number.'

In the hyper-analytical world of Harvard, where dating often appeared to be yet another strategic enterprise worthy of a spreadsheet, it was wonderful to meet the woman I would marry in such a love-at-first-sight way. Katie is from the American Midwest, and she still finds some of my English mannerisms curious. But, of course, she understands me, despite that dramatic introduction, better than anyone else. Her number was the one piece of data that I'll always be grateful to Harvard for. I hesitate to use it to prove a point, but if I were to suggest one it would be this: I'm not sure I believe in fate, exactly, but I do think that if you are true to yourself, life occasionally presents you with the opportunities you have been waiting for. After that, the rest is up to you.

My experience at Harvard contributed to the creation and philosophy of Tough Mudder in a crucial way. It taught me quite a few things that I did not want to be: things that perhaps should have indicated to me far earlier that I had gone there for the wrong reasons. I did not want to work in a consultancy. I did not want to work in finance. I had no wish to go along with a culture that treated success as a zero-sum game. For me to succeed, you have to fail. I did, however, come away with a strong belief that there were plenty of other people out there who thought like me. They were people who craved belonging and purpose at least as much as money and status, who wanted to be part of something that they could believe in. If I hadn't really found that belief at Harvard, I had found the space to develop the idea that there was a kind of business that could be attractive to those people. Tough Mudder was designed to prove those beliefs. It was also created, I think, because having exhausted all available options of tribes and cultures I might fit into, the time had come to create one of my own.

It is, of course, no accident that those ideas are built into the events themselves. I like to believe that Tough Mudders value a different kind of winning from that which is still seen on Wall Street and beyond. Tough Mudders are encouraged to see the event – and life – as a challenge and not a race. They are not only interested in rankings. Instead, they have become a global movement of achievers who believe in the value of a communal spirit rather than in dog-eat-dog competition, who want to test their limits but are more concerned with 'we' than with 'I'.

In life, as in business, the meeting of opposites is productive. A rival can help you show what you might be capable of. One of the most fortunate breaks we had at the beginning of Tough Mudder was that it was immediately presented with its perfect mirror image. A bad cop to our good cop. Just at the moment that I created Tough Mudder with all these ideas in my head about meeting individual goals as part of a group, a rival obstacle event that professed exactly the opposite set of values was also starting out.

That event, Spartan Race, was – naturally – created by a former Wall Street equities trader called Joe De Sena, then in his early forties. De Sena, a native of Queens, New York, looked a lot like the living embodiment of the deeply competitive winner-takes-all ideal that Wall Street represented, and so did his event.

Joe is, by his own admission, a man who likes nothing better than to prove he can carry a canoe up a mountain and that you can't.

He wakes in the morning and moves large rocks around to show he is still able to. 'If you put a gun to my head,' he says, 'and asked me what I love to do, I would say I love torturing myself and I love torturing other people.' Spartan Race is based on his philosophy that success is earned through punishment and self-denial. It celebrates the idea that in life there can only ever be one winner and that ruthless competitiveness is the best way to ensure that the winner is you. De Sena likes to say that if two sisters come to a Spartan Race for a laugh, by the second obstacle, they will be doing their utmost to leave their sibling behind in the mud. You will rarely see any Spartan stop to help a fellow Spartan over an obstacle – the fundamental experience on a Tough Mudder course – and anyone who fails to get over Spartan obstacles is punished by having to perform multiple numbers of burpees, De Sena's favourite squat jump.

In many ways, De Sena's race was a kind of godsend for Tough Mudder. From the beginning, and in all things, we wanted to demonstrate that we were not Spartan Race. That although, like Joe De Sena, we believed in hard challenges as a route to personal achievement, unlike him, we did not believe in punishments and humiliation. We wanted to show that a tribal spirit of cooperation would prove more attractive than a message of 'win at all costs'. And also that it would result in more creative energy around obstacles and innovation, as well as a stronger business. Grit and character may have been qualities to develop in yourself, but you discovered them most enjoyably not in solitary achievement but in collaborative effort.

To the arch-competitor in Joe De Sena, that obviously all sounded like fighting talk. Not long after we started out we began to discover Spartan spies skulking around in the undergrowth the night before Tough Mudder events, photographing us setting up and taking notes on changes to our obstacles. Having been involved in more serious undercover operations myself in the past, it was quite hard not to laugh and also to respond a little in kind. The rivalry was fuelled, as both companies grew, by a series of magazine articles that deliberately stoked it.

'There's not a person on this planet I despise more than Will Dean,' said Joe De Sena in one of them. 'Every day I wake up just out of spite for the guy.'

It was clear we had got to him. 'It wasn't about money any more,' he said, 'or being successful. I wanted to win because I wanted to beat these English guys, college kids. It was like *First Blood* for me.'

The more determined to beat us Joe got and the more popular Tough Mudder became in relation to Spartan Race, the more fun we had thinking of ways to wind him up. For a man who cared a lot about being first, being second was probably not to his liking.

'I think Joe De Sena and I have a lot in common,' I told one journalist. 'Every morning I wake up thinking about the success of Tough Mudder, and every morning so does he.'

We used to spend a bit of time after hours in the early days at TMHQ in Brooklyn creating what we called Spartan disruption. We organized a plane to fly over the second ever Spartan Race trailing the banner 'You think this is tough? You should try Tough Mudder.' We guessed that De Sena would respond to this challenge by hiring planes to fly over every single one of our events that year. I also knew that to hire a plane for the afternoon cost fifteen thousand dollars. He took the bait. Every time a plane flew over a Tough Mudder race that summer I would smile and think about Joe De Sena's bottom line.

We had a series of occasions in which we ended up scheduling events in the same state on the same weekend, mostly I think by chance (although not in Joe's eyes). He accused someone in our office of sending him a copy of *How to Win Friends and Influence People* in the mail. He seemed to get really mad when he first discovered a hack that we'd made that caused a Tough Mudder ad to flash up every time someone clicked on the Spartan Facebook page. Fearing a bit for Joe's blood pressure, Guy and I arranged to have lunch with him, as a peace offering. He came, pumped, to the New York restaurant, in wraparound shades and shorts, but after a predictably friendly chat, and some swapping of war stories, the rivalry cooled down a little, and after that existed mainly in the pages of magazines.

These days we both realize there is plenty of room for both events, and that there are plenty of things that we share – Joe, like me, has the very positive desire to get people off the sofa and doing challenging things with each other out of doors and building some grit and character along the way – even if there are fundamental philosophies about achieving those ends that we disagree on. It is remarkable how much people have taken those differences to heart: surprisingly few people cross from one event to the other. In the way that people are givers or takers, believers or cynics, you are broadly either a Mudder or a Spartan, and the world produces plenty of both. De Sena even admitted recently, 'I have to say the fact that Will Dean has stuck it out despite what we threw at him is impressive. You know even in war adversaries start to have some kind of fondness for each other. Fight somebody long enough and hard enough and you can't help having a little respect for them.'

I probably won't stop pointing out who is winning the war Joe believes he is engaged in, but I'm also happy to admit that the respect is entirely mutual.

MUDDER GRIT: Deanna Blegg

You can't stand and watch a Tough Mudder, let alone take part in one, without becoming absorbed by the question of what exactly it is that keeps people going through the mud and ice and water when every cell in their bodies appears to be screaming at them to quit. One answer to that question is that each Mudder takes inspiration from all those other Mudders around them: if they can do it, so can I. Character becomes infectious. We literally draw strength from each other.

Few people have ever disregarded the screaming of their bodies to stop – and in this way offered as much strength to others on the Mudder course – as Deanna Blegg. Deanna ran our first Australian Tough Mudder in Victoria in 2012. The following year, at age forty-three, she completed an extraordinary eighty-five Mudder miles in twenty-four hours to become the women's World's Toughest Mudder in New Jersey. But those facts don't begin to tell her story. If anyone embodied our spirit of keep on keeping on, of the grit involved in moving forward and never looking back, it's Deanna.

In some ways, Deanna says, she feels she was born to be a Tough Mudder. She grew up in the Dandenong Ranges outside Melbourne, her home backing onto a national park, and she and her sister and their dog were out trail running – often by moonlight – from a very early age. As a teenager, all sports came quite naturally to her, but she had no interest in committing to one thing. She never had any formal coaching or was part of any clubs because she just liked to train when the mood struck her, but at sixteen she was Australian cross-country champion for her age group, and by the age of twenty-two she was a member of the Australian Pro Triathlon team for the world championships.

It was a couple of years after that that Deanna's life hit its first major obstacle. While travelling in Europe, Deanna was infected with HIV by her then boyfriend. This was 1994 and, when she received the news, the diagnosis was bleak. There was no medication available and an awful lot of stigma and fear experienced by those who contracted the virus. The doctor told Deanna if she lasted five years, that would be considered long term. 'I remember even discussing with him the places that allowed euthanasia,' Deanna recalls now. 'I didn't want to have that slow crappy thing. So I just thought, *well, we'll find what country allows me to slip off pretty quick.*'

It didn't come to that. The antiretroviral drugs that were developed held Deanna's symptoms in check and, partly to escape what she saw as the ugliness of the virus, she went on travelling, as far and wide as possible. These adventures took another horrific turn in 1995, however, when she was on the road with her cousin in Ethiopia. The two of them were taken hostage by a militia group. In a shoot-out that followed, Deanna was wounded, but her cousin was killed. 'That was a very, very rough time in my life,' she says. It was also the end of her travelling. She returned to Australia, settled down, had a couple of kids, and concentrated on trying to keep well and safe, advocating for openness in talking about living with HIV, something she had struggled with for a decade.

By the time she reached her mid-thirties Deanna's athletic promise was long forgotten. Then one day in 2005 she picked up a flyer for an adventure race that involved a combination of running, swimming, paddling and mountain biking. She told her then partner: 'I'm going to win this.' He had never known Deanna as an athlete, so he just looked at her and smiled: 'Yeah, right.' So determined was she to get fit that year, though, that Deanna made the mistake of skipping some of her drugs and ended up in the hospital with full-blown AIDS. Her doctors told her not to exercise too much, but once she was back at home she continued with her plan to compete in the race. When she finally did, she says, 'All that passion and love and enthusiasm that I had had previously as a kid came back – and that was it.' She picked up her training. 'I kept building it up bit by bit,' she says, 'and I was getting my bloods done and my immune system checked and not surprisingly, the fitter I became the stronger my immune system got.'

Deanna was forty-two when she heard on the radio that Tough Mudder was coming to Australia. 'My immediate thought was not only to experience it but to get round in the top 5 per cent so I could go to World's Toughest Mudder.'

She's still never had a routine for her training. 'I look outside and if it's a beautiful day, I think, *There's a trail outside my door; let's see what happens*.' And, just like when she was a girl, she still runs in the middle of the night. 'If the moon allows it, I won't go out with a headlight,' she says. 'Your senses become very attuned to the surroundings, little noises, and I'm sure my heart rate increases. Everything is very heightened: you feel at one, animalistic.'

When she got to World's Toughest Mudder for the second time in 2014, all that night running proved invaluable. Deanna ran her eighty-five miles even though as the run went on she developed a fear of the Cliff Jump – thirty feet into the lake in the dark – after a bad landing on a previous lap. At one point she stood for around twenty minutes in the moonlight contemplating the drop.

Of her determination, she says, 'I think I've developed an ability to just switch my brain off. I'm not a person that worries too much. The shooting in Ethiopia was on replay in my head for a while. But I'm like, how do I begin to move on from this, the best way I can? That's my approach with everything.'

When she went to her first World's Toughest Mudder, Deanna had no idea how far she would go. Her goal was just to keep moving. When she's running she doesn't let any excuses interfere with her motivation. She doesn't think for twenty-four hours. 'If you asked me straight after the race what obstacle followed what obstacle,' she says, 'I don't think I'd be able to tell you.' In a life in which bad surprises have often been waiting around the corner, she tries to live in the moment.

As a determinedly solitary runner (apart from the company of her dog), Deanna found the camaraderie of Tough Mudder at first unusual and then exhilarating. 'I always liked my own company,' she says. 'But I discovered I also like experiencing and being a part of what is not familiar to me, which is that team and that sense of being part of a community. That's become very important to me.'

All the more so now, because in the summer of 2016, Deanna was diagnosed with breast cancer, and at the time of writing she is in the middle of chemotherapy. She has approached her treatment the way she has learned to approach everything: always looking to take on the next thing in her way and then the one after that. 'There is no option other than the chemo, so I don't stress about it,' she says, 'I don't fight it. I'm not fighting cancer either; I've accepted it and I am going through the process of giving my body the best opportunity and the chance to be strong through it. I had a bout of pneumonia to begin with, so that knocked me back, but I'm still training when I can. There are some times when I can only walk during the day but other than that I will run or I will ride. And I'm sleeping a lot.'

The community of obstacle racers and Tough Mudders 'have just been beautiful' through all this, Deanna says. A charity was started in her name with the proper Tough Mudder moniker: #fuckityfuckit cancer. Runners across the world have been buying pink wristbands to support it all year, and muddy photos and messages from wristband wearers have been flooding Deanna's Facebook page. When her friends ask Deanna about her prospects for running World's Toughest Mudder in 2017, she answers the same way she has always answered, with all the cheerful grit she can muster: 'All going well I'll be there.' No one doubts it.

CHAPTER 3

'I Do Not Whine – Kids Whine': Owning Your Fears

I learned that courage was not the absence of fear but the triumph over it.

– Nelson Mandela

The ritual we created for the starting line of Tough Mudder has evolved a lot from the wild *Braveheart* charge of the first event. It is still designed to deliver a major shot of adrenaline, just in a slightly more predictable fashion. It is there to put Mudders in the frame of mind for whatever new thing the course can throw at them, designed to summon that ancient emotion: courage. It always seems worth remembering that the root of that word is the Latin *cor*, meaning 'heart'. To display courage was always both to put your full heart into something and to feel the blood pumping madly in your veins as a result. Our bodies crave that feeling, but how often, these days, do we get to experience it?

Our 'legionnaires', or returning Mudders, have gone through the starting line ritual before and will have some painful or triumphant memories of obstacles such as Everest – the greasy half-pipe they must run up with the help of other Mudders – or Electroshock Therapy – the net of hanging live wires that can deliver ten thousand volts of electricity. New Mudders will almost certainly be wary or possibly completely terrified. Tough Mudder is not an event that you can ever be confident in advance that you can complete, like a 10K or a marathon. But everyone will be full of adrenaline and high on risk. There is, in any case, no turning back now.

The atmosphere at a Tough Mudder is somewhere between the physical seriousness of an Iron Man and the alternative cultishness of Burning Man, with a bit of village carnival thrown in. I've been to hundreds of events since that first one at Bear Creek, but the sense of expectation at the starting line and of achievement at the finish still always get to me. Though Tough Mudders in different countries each have their own culture, there is a common spirit that runs through all our events. We want a festival feeling – ten thousand individuals gathered in a field in sun or rain (or hail and snow) bringing their whole selves. But we also want a real sense of anticipation of the genuine test of courage and commitment about to take place.

We designed the Tough Mudder's staggered start to create both intimacy and belonging. I'm a believer in Dunbar's number – research by the Oxford University professor Robin Dunbar that shows that the strongest communities are created in groups of around 150. Any more than that and you don't recognize every face; any fewer and there is not enough diversity. It's one reason we divide the thousands of Mudders at any given event into smaller groups. We don't want people to feel like another anonymous face in the crowd as they might at a big city marathon. Every fifteen minutes on a Tough Mudder weekend another hundred or so participants have a high-energy aerobic workout. And then they run up an eight-foot wall, a minor taste of things to come – which they hopefully clamber over without too much difficulty (if not, they really are in trouble) – before listening to some words of inspiration about what lies ahead. Some Mudders are friends; most are strangers. By the time they set off to run up the first hill, the idea is that they do not feel that they are in this alone.

It's always fascinating to watch these groups. Some people are in fancy dress; many are running for a cause or for a loved one. Most people are gym fit, whereas a few have clearly done most of their training on a sofa in front of a TV. There are groups of college friends, work colleagues, classmates on a reunion, sports teams, neighbours, extended families, running partners, a few wiry pensioners. Once they get over that first wall though, they are suddenly pretty much on a level. You watch people at the starting line instinctively scanning the smiles of the people around them, building trust. Bouncing on their toes, expectant and alert. Tough Mudder is not an event you can do, or would ever want to do, wearing earbuds and an iPhone – though quite a few wear head cameras to capture their own adventure.

In the beginning, Tough Mudder employees delivered the pledge speech that starts each race. My friend Alex Patterson, who joined us after the first event as our general counsel and subsequently filled just about every role in the company, had a particularly energetic sideline in beatboxing and one-handed push-ups. These days we employ MCs to deliver the Mudder starting line message.

Sean Corvelle has been our main American MC for five years now. He has all the fervour of a southern preacher and the conviction of a drill sergeant, with a fair bit of authentic Mudder mischief thrown in. He is also the accepted grand master of the tribal shout of Tough Mudders everywhere: HOO-RAH! His five-minute performance is not a regular motivational speech. It's an evangelical sermon, and a renegade rap, a call to arms and a pledge of purpose.

'Welcome to what we call possibly the toughest event on the planet. Are you ready for this?'

'Hoo-rah!'

'I said, ARE YOU READY?'

'HOO-RAH!'

'What we have for you today is ten miles of total hell designed by British Special Forces! Who is up for a proper challenge?'

'HOO-RAH!'

'Who is going to have an orange headband at the end of the day? I wanna hear you!'

'HOO-RAH!'

'We are testing your fitness, your stamina, your teamwork, your mental grit. Who has mental grit?'

'HOO-RAH!'

'Remember, you are looking out for each other. You come across any obstacle you are not feeling, you go around it. If you cannot swim, do not go in the water. Make sure someone sees you go in, make sure you see your friends come out.'

'HOO-RAH!'

'This is your family today. Are we a team?'

'HOO-RAH!'

From the beginning, in particular in America, Tough Mudder has had strong support from active-duty soldiers, and in turn has linked with veterans' charities. In our first five years our participants were the biggest single donors to the Wounded Warrior charity for disabled veterans of the wars in Iraq and Afghanistan. From 2016, we have been partnered with Team Rubicon, the charity that sends veterans to help in disaster relief. Every starting line group at our events in the United States will contain both veterans and people running for veterans' charities – it's pretty much the same in the United Kingdom and elsewhere. Sean makes special mention of this fact. As well as the HOO-RAHs there will usually be ten seconds of silence for wounded and fallen friends before a rousing chorus of 'The Stars and Stripes Forever' and the collective shout of the Tough Mudder pledge: 'As a Tough Mudder I understand Tough Mudder is not a race but a challenge. I put teamwork and camaraderie before my course time. I do not whine – kids whine . . .'

Sean then rises to his crescendo. 'Look each other in the eye. Today these are your brothers and sisters!'

'HOO-RAH!'

'Give a hug to someone behind you or next to you. Because as Tough Mudders we leave no Mudders behind; everyone makes it to the finish! You are all awesome! You are all Tough Mudders!'

'HOO-RAH!'

And then the countdown begins, and with a final wild 'HOO-RAH!' the Mudders set off towards their first challenge.

Courage comes in many forms. One of the great privileges of my role at Tough Mudder is that I have been able to witness many of them. There is the obvious courage of the Tough Mudder legends celebrated in this book – the courage of Deanna Blegg, for example. But though they display heart on a level most of us can only begin to imagine, I think every one of our participants displays a degree of courage just to be on that starting line. As the psychologist Brené Brown observes in her book *Daring Greatly*, 'Courage starts with turning up and letting ourselves be seen.' Courage lies in Mudders' commitment to lose some weight and get themselves into shape for the event or to be prepared to be at least a bit humiliated in front of their friends, to risk falling flat on their face in a muddy bog or a loss of nerve at Arctic Enema – our Jacuzzi full of ice – and come out smiling. Courage exposes your willingness to prove your worth by doing something that is beyond your normal experience. All of us have a sense of our limitations. Not all of us can always find the heart to try to go beyond them.

In some ways, in my own experience, I think there is no better examination of these facts than setting out on your own to try to make a success of a business or other enterprise. Many people think that they would like to start out on their own, but only a few have the conviction to do so. In comparison to a Mudder challenge, founding a company is quite a lonely and sometimes scary place to be. There is generally no starting line or motivational speech to get you ready for what lies ahead. I had one or two people encouraging me when I started Tough Mudder, but most of the voices around me were cautionary or worse. People who write about entrepreneurs talk a lot about a capacity for risk, but the real quality that unites the successful entrepreneurs I have known is the courage just to get going – and the resilience that makes you continue where others might give up. I believe that, like any other quality, courage can be learned and earned, but it comes through an initial determination to stretch yourself, to put yourself on the line. 'Your time is limited,' Steve Jobs said. 'So don't waste it living someone else's life. Don't be trapped by dogma – which is living with the results of other people's thinking. Don't let the noise of others' opinions drown out your own inner voice. And most important, have the courage to follow your heart and intuition.'

What Steve Jobs didn't say, but what his life story often proved, was that any risk meets obstacles. The thing about life, and about business, is that however hard you prepare for it, however ready you make yourself, there will be plenty waiting around the corner to derail you. Tough Mudder as an event dramatizes that fact: it is about expecting the unexpected, about owning your fears.

We are all defined in the end by how we cope with adversity. It is for that reason when any of us look back over our lives we tend to remember not the simple successes but the near disasters that we have overcome. At Tough Mudder we have had our fair share of war stories. There was the time when Superstorm Sandy hit New York City in 2012. Our water-facing warehouse in the Brooklyn Army Terminal, containing all our gear, was completely flooded. The surging water ripped the metal gates off their hinges and the river streamed in. We spent a day in the driving rain and gales trying to fish boxes of T-shirts out of the swollen river, wash them in batches at the laundromat, and repackage them for the drive down to Florida for our final event of the season. At the same time the apartment building I lived in was also flooded – we had no water or electricity for three weeks, and we had to walk up twelve flights of stairs every day. The Tough Mudder office building was under three feet of water, along with almost every other building on our block in the newly cool DUMBO – Down Under the Manhattan Bridge Overpass – district in which we were then based. Hundreds of multicoloured cupcakes floated down the street after escaping from one of the washed-out hipster coffee shops.

Floods were by no means the only act of God. Our event at Cedartown in rural Georgia in 2011 was to be held at a local motocross track. We had received our alcohol licence several months in advance of the event only to have a local Baptist minister whip up the locals into a fervour about 'metrosexuals' and hippies from

Atlanta and beyond invading their dry county to wallow in mud and drink beer on the Sabbath. The chief of police and the mayor knew our event was quite valuable economically to the poor rural community and that we wouldn't be returning the following year if they revoked our licence, but nonetheless they weren't prepared to back us against such an influential local constituent as the evangelical church.

I was summoned to a town hall meeting, where I was greeted by an angry mob quoting scripture and carrying placards about Tough Mudder being the work of the devil. For some reason the locals seemed to believe I was both German and the Antichrist. I was not only advocating drinking alcohol on the Sabbath but I was also clearly the worst kind of foreigner. If they'd had pitchforks on hand, I have little doubt I would have been run out of town. The alcohol licence was not granted. But the event went ahead. And, of course, in the end people brought their own beer and drank a lot more of it than they might have done otherwise.

These kinds of unexpected dramas happened almost every month in our first few years. But the first, and in many ways the toughest obstacle the business – and I personally – had to face, the biggest test of our Mudder courage, occurred exactly a week after that opening event in Allentown, when in our makeshift office in Brooklyn, I was served a writ by an eighty-year-old army veteran called Billy Wilson from Wolverhampton, England. This fact, and the long saga that resulted from it, became a kind of ongoing nightmare for me and for the company. I had a habit of telling the team back then that we were in our own version of *Fight Club* – collectively committed to creating an underground adventure that hadn't previously existed. If you know that movie, you will understand me when I say our encounter with Billy Wilson threatened to turn that *Fight Club* into Project Mayhem and bring everything that we had built crashing down.

Wilson is a man who dresses in antique military uniforms – in memory of his national service sixty years ago – has a handlebar moustache, and likes to call himself Mr Mouse, with a measure of irony. He is not a timid individual. Mr Mouse had established an obstacle event in 1986 in Wolverhampton, England, and he was, the writ informed me, suing Tough Mudder, then only a week or so old. He had filed a multimillion-dollar civil suit in a district court against us claiming breach of contract and violation of trade secrets, among other charges.

I'd had the briefest of histories with Mr Mouse eighteen months earlier. When I was preparing my Harvard Business School start-up plan for an obstacle event marketed at scale, I had taken the opportunity to visit the two closest cousins of the idea that were up and running in Europe. The first was an event called Strongman Run in Germany. It was, bizarrely, used as a promotional tool for the extra-strong type of British throat lozenge called Fisherman's Friend. In Britain, these lozenges were the kind of thing that your granddad might keep in his coat pocket. In Germany, with a smart bit of re-branding, they were being sold in nightclubs and at raves as head-clearing party sweets. They were the Red Bull of throat lozenges. And the Strongman Run event was a spin-off to promote that idea.

I was fascinated both by the success of this event and the weirdness of the business model. Though ten thousand people invariably signed up to participate on the day Strongman Run was announced, the Fisherman's Friend people were charging a nominal fifteen-euro fee and using the event itself as a loss leader. It was clear to me that people would pay much more to do the Strongman Run, which they loved. I had some discussion with the marketing group behind the event, suggesting they would be better off being an obstacle event company who gave away throat lozenges rather than a throat lozenge company that gave away obstacle events. They weren't convinced, but for a while the CEO, who had done the German rebranding of Fisherman's Friend, was intrigued enough to offer to invest in our early Tough Mudder concept. I offered him 10 per cent of the company for two hundred thousand dollars. He agreed at first, but in the end he decided to stick to throat sweets (and many other repackaged export brands). It was his loss: his stake would now be worth many multiples of that original investment. I saw him when we started Tough Mudder in Germany and he could smile about it. The problem had been, he said, that there was no market in America for Fisherman's Friend lozenges.

In many ways, the German Strongman Run was closer to my eventual ideas for Tough Mudder than the other event I looked at, in Britain. Mr Mouse had been running Tough Guy on his farm near Wolverhampton in the English Midlands (about fifty miles from where I grew up) for twenty years when I went to see him. It was a one-off midwinter mud run that involved twenty-five obstacles. It had grown over the years through word of mouth to attract five thousand participants.

I killed an hour at his local pub before driving out to see him, and contemplated turning around and going home. In hindsight, I wish I had. But I had arranged to see him to talk about Tough Guy, perhaps use it as a reference point in my Harvard business plan, and in return maybe offer him a bit of free MBA consultancy about how his business strategy might be improved. It would be rude not to turn up. I also had a vague thought that if I found Mr Mouse someone to do business with, there might be a way of licensing the Tough Guy name in the States and repackaging the concept (much in the way that Fisherman's Friend had gone to Germany).

Mr Mouse was an interesting character. His farm was advertised as a donkey sanctuary. When I tried to talk to him in any detail about the lucrative business he had made of Tough Guy, he replied mostly with his philosophy about the competitive nature of life and his own role in it.

I did honour my part of our agreement, though, and sent Mr Mouse a brief paper about how he might expand his business or export the concept. He, of course, had no patent on obstacle courses – they were as old as the hills. There were two aspects of my dealings with him that I later came to regret. The first was to sign a non-disclosure agreement on arrival. The second was that in creating our first website I had used a couple of photos from Tough Guy along with pictures from other mud events, like Strongman Run, captioned 'for illustrative purposes only'. Both of these featured in the multimillion-dollar lawsuit.

On top of that, Mr Mouse contacted Harvard Business School, alleging that I had met him under false pretences and stolen his idea. The timing of those allegations was unfortunate. They came in the wake of the Enron scandal that had involved several Harvard Business School graduates – Jeff Skilling had recently been sentenced to twenty-four years in prison – not to mention the 2008 banking crisis that in the popular mind was attributed to the behaviour of other HBS alumni on Wall Street. The Business School, like any corporate organization, was worried for its reputation, which was, increasingly, one of being a hothouse for unscrupulous alpha males who would stop at nothing to enrich themselves.

So in 2010, any mention of business ethics set alarm bells ringing. And here was an eighty-year-old Englishman alleging unethical behaviour from me. It looked like an opportunity for the faculty to take a stand. An opportunity, moreover, that didn't involve any downside for Harvard itself. It wasn't as if they would be reprimanding an alumnus in one of the banks or corporations that sponsored HBS professors on consultancy projects or speaking engagements. Nor were they risking any of the relationships that guaranteed that HBS graduates strolled into prestigious roles on Wall Street or in Silicon Valley. Instead, they would be making a stand against a recent graduate working from a borrowed desk in the corner of a warehouse in DUMBO.

As a result of the letter I was summoned before a court of academics – a Conduct Review Board – to answer Mr Mouse's claims. My initial instinct was not to attend. I had left the university, and I felt that Mr Mouse's dispute was now a matter for the US legal system rather than an ad hoc group of academics. Katie, among others, advised that I should go along and submit to Harvard's process to put that part of the matter to rest. I knew my actions amounted to nothing more than checking out the market before starting a business. Having witnessed some of the faculty's defensiveness firsthand, I was suspicious of the process, however. I wasn't wrong.

A sketchy 'enquiry' had apparently taken place. A month after I had given my side of the story the review board ruled that although 'there was insufficient evidence that [William Dean] inappropriately used confidential information . . . provided by Tough Guy Limited in developing his own enterprise', I had, apparently, 'violated standards of HBS integrity' in my dealings with Mr Mouse. The board recommended placing me on 'alumni probation' for five years.

The pomposity of that judgement sounds quite amusing in retrospect. At the time, though, I was hurt and angry that Harvard felt any sanction was justified. I was naive in underestimating the fear of reputational damage in large organizations. I don't care too much about what other people think of me, but I have a strong sense of personal right and wrong. Here I was, while the world was engulfed in ever more scandalous tales of unethical business practices at the highest levels of Wall Street, scapegoated for some trivial transgression in trying to set up a mud-run event on Facebook.

As I said at the outset of this chapter, courage comes in many forms. The legal situation with Mr Mouse seemed to require a particular version of it. From my Foreign Office days, I was used to situations in which it was not advisable to take a step back or to show weakness. I had learned not to bury fears and even paranoia but instead to separate them into rational components and face them head-on. But none of that seemed much use in this opaque, strangely one-sided, slightly ludicrous battle in which I wanted no part but couldn't avoid.

I had assumed – since I had clearly broken no law and there was no damage to Mr Mouse's business in England by our setting up Tough Mudder in America – that the case would be thrown out of court. I quickly came to discover that is not quite how the American legal system works. To get to the point where the case was dismissed we had to employ a lawyer. I set up a meeting with a New York City firm. They asked for a five hundred thousand dollar retainer at our first meeting and suggested that if the case went to court, it would cost two million dollars whatever the verdict.

We obviously could not afford those fees, but we had to defend the case. I'm a great believer that there is always a solution to any problem if you look at it long enough, but this time I looked hard and long and couldn't see one. I'm a pretty good sleeper, but now I was lying awake in the early hours rolling the details of the case around in my mind. During the days in the office and at events it seemed that Tough Mudder was developing as we had always hoped. But at three a.m. it often felt all we were working for could be destroyed by this legal case.

Alex Patterson, our beat-boxing general counsel, came up with the way forward. Alex had gone earlier that year and run the Tough Guy event – on a cold and dreary January day in Wolverhampton – so he had seen firsthand what we were up against. His solution was both simple and welcome. While at Harvard he had helped to establish an unlikely Ivy League surfing competition with a former lifeguard buddy, Matt Siben. Matt had subsequently become a leading New York trial attorney. Relying on old surfers' camaraderie, Alex managed to persuade Matt to take our case virtually pro bono. Matt approached Mr Mouse in classic New York lawyerly spirit: 'We'll depose the arse off him.'

On Matt's advice, we counter-sued for defamation. Mr Mouse in turn had hired an American attorney who happened to have competed in the Tough Guy event and was just starting out in a career in San Diego.

There were a few comic interludes in what became a long and draining battle. In 2011, a team from the Tough Mudder office ran an event at a new venue at a very-high-altitude ski mountain in California. On that Saturday the weather was fine, but on Sunday, when we were due to run, there was a sudden snowstorm and the temperature had dropped to minus fifteen degrees. It became by far the toughest event we had ever staged. We had put the Arctic Enema very near the start of the course, and half the participants dropped out after that obstacle. The Tough Mudder team, myself included, felt obliged to carry on. My knee got frostbitten, and the only way to avoid hypothermia at the far end of the course was to run wrapped in two or three silver-foil sheets. I remember jumping into the pond at the top of the mountain, and although the water had been fifty degrees at most, it felt as if I had landed in a warm bath. By the end, we were all sore and relieved – and shivering uncontrollably for hours afterwards.

The next day we were due to meet Wilson's lawyer in San Diego. Our legs were cut up and bruised to the extent that we couldn't put on jeans and had to wear loose shorts. Our faces were so windburned that we looked like we had just returned from a polar expedition. When we limped into the lawyers' office every face said 'What the hell happened to you?' and 'Do we really want to take on these guys in a courtroom?'

Another time, at the height of my parents' anxiety about Mr Mouse, some packages arrived unexpectedly at their house in Worksop: four large boxes addressed to me and delivered by a male courier with what sounded like a Wolverhampton accent. My sister called to ask me what the packages were. I said I didn't know anything about any large packages and suggested she and the rest of the family leave them untouched on the driveway until I could get up there from London. By the time I arrived, I had become convinced the boxes were a new part of Mr Mouse's tactics. I poked at one tentatively with a broom handle and saw some packaging that I tried to decipher at arm's length. The boxes, it turned out, were full of Highland toffee bars that I had agreed to take over to New York as a favour to a friend who gave them out to clients at Christmas. Bomb disposal was not required.

The best strategy when you are playing chicken is to rip the steering wheel out of your car and toss it out of the window. Knowing you have no control, your opponent has no option but to swerve. By the time of the toffee bar incident, I had decided that on no account was I going to let Mr Mouse intimidate me. I hadn't asked for a fight but I wasn't going to flinch.

Still, I found myself increasingly distracted by it all. I would wake up on a Saturday morning next to Katie and the sun would be shining, and for about seven seconds all was right with the world and then I would think: *Fuck . . . the lawsuit.* It followed me everywhere. As press about Tough Mudder increased, it started to become part of the narrative about me: the easy story was that I had stolen the business of an eighty-year-old. Journalists had the Harvard 'alumni sanction' to back them up. The hard part was trying to correct it. Tough Mudder was growing faster than we could have hoped – we were spreading our message to a loyal tribe – but there was always the threat on the horizon that the lawsuit could destroy it all.

In the end, it was Guy who persuaded me that we had to somehow end the process of claim and counterclaim and get into a courtroom and, whatever the rights and wrongs, make some kind of settlement. He feared it was not only taking up too much of our time but also making me ill. Katie agreed. I reluctantly took their advice, and a date was set for a hearing in the Brooklyn courthouse just around the corner from where Katie and I lived, and which I cycled past on my way to the office every morning.

We were lucky to have been assigned a very patient judge, who, after having heard the claims, suggested that either we would both be liable for the legal costs, or – and this is what he strongly recommended – we go outside and mediate a settlement.

As our lawyers argued about appropriate mediation, it was suggested that Mr Mouse and I meet for a drink to try to iron out our differences and come to an agreement. He was staying at an old-fashioned New York hotel in Midtown and appeared in its gloomy bar at the appointed hour. Our lawyers were standing nearby, making sure we remained civilized.

When I left the bar, without any agreement, Guy and Alex were waiting around the corner. They say I met them with a strange unfocused stare. That I looked emotionally exhausted. I've been through some tough stuff in my life, but even on assignment chasing terrorists for the Foreign Office, I can honestly say I never felt more drained.

Guy and Matt and Alex argued that we make one final monetary offer. Extremely reluctantly I agreed; and even more reluctantly, it appeared, so did Mr Mouse, and he accepted our offer.

The publicity around the case follows me around. I was questioned about it on CBS's *60 Minutes* and on the BBC, where I was described hilariously as 'the Mark Zuckerberg of obstacle racing', as well as in the *New Yorker*, *The New York Times* and in a long profile piece in *Outside* magazine.

The *Outside* profile whipped up our legal case into a full-scale blood feud. It portrayed me as a 'cut-throat entrepreneur', a 'polished Englishman and Harvard Business School grad who will stop at nothing to sell you his brand of suffering', accusing me of 'playing dirty', among other things.

The episode with Mr Mouse taught me one or two hard lessons. The first one was that you can't control what people say about you or think about you, but you can control how you react – at which point being honest with yourself about your actions and motivations becomes the only thing that counts. 'Truth and courage aren't always comfortable,' the psychologist Brené Brown argues, 'but they're never weakness.'

We live in an online world where opinions are cheap and often anonymous. When you get negative publicity that you believe unfair, the day afterwards you feel, 'God, what will everyone think of me?' Then you realize that the people who know you will think exactly the same of you as they did before. And the people who don't know you, you're not too concerned about anyway. That knowledge is liberating.

You also realize that people who don't know you much prefer caricatures to reality. In my case, it seems to be 'Harvard grad and unscrupulous'.

If I am ever interviewed in the press or on TV, I always know that somewhere along the line the journalist will ask, 'How do you feel about being called "the Mark Zuckerberg of extreme sports"?'

I reply that I think it's very flattering.

They say, 'No, I think the comparison is meant not in a good way; it's about stealing Mr Mouse's idea.'

I say, 'That's not what happened and that's not the way I take it.'

Defensiveness can become a bad habit, but there is no requirement to apologize for things you haven't done wrong. As Mark Zuckerberg was supposed to have said to the Winklevoss twins, who accused him in court of stealing their idea: 'If you guys were the inventors of Facebook, you'd have invented Facebook.' I felt the same way about Tough Mudder.

The other lesson I learned is that old favourite: that adversity always has its uses. If the lawsuit from Mr Mouse had not occurred in those first days of the company, I doubt Tough Mudder would ever have been half as successful as it quickly became. We learned fast that we had to fight for what we had started and for what we believed in. No one was going to give us an easy ride. The facts of the case and the criticism also sharpened our belief in what we were trying to create. It hardened our resolve to make the Tough Mudder community authentically generous and courageous in spirit and action, proof that we were never the cut-throat capitalists that some of that criticism implied. Another result was that I worked like a maniac for nearly three years to grow the company partly because I was absolutely determined that the lawsuit would not destroy us. Nothing focuses your mind more on what you have than the imminent prospect of losing it all, particularly if that threat is the result of an injustice. In the early years of Tough Mudder, that was an ever-present anxiety. But the threats didn't kill us. They ultimately made us stronger.

MUDDER COURAGE: Randy Pierce

Legend has it that the Emperor Charlemagne used to watch his foot soldiers closely when they came to a river to set up camp after another long day's march. Some of his men unpacked their gear, dug out a flask, and knelt at the edge of the river to fill it to take a drink. Others just took one look at the river, let out a roar, and dived straight in. These were the men the general always knew that he wanted beside him in the battles to come.

When we started Tough Mudder seven years ago, it was with something like that idea in mind. There is a lot of planning in our lives, a great deal of risk management and careful examination of options. These habits are useful in their place. But there are many moments in life when they are not enough. If you want to discover what you are capable of, or challenge yourself to take a big step forward in your life, no cost–benefit analysis or pros and cons list will tell you what to do. Sometimes the only answer is to go to the edge of the river, take the risk of diving in, and accept the consequences.

This courage to take a leap into the unknown is the basis of many of our obstacles. For me, one moment embodies that ethos best: Randy Pierce's jump on King of the Swingers in Los Angeles in 2015.

Randy lost most of his sight at age twenty-two in 1989 to a rare neurological disease, and he went completely blind in 2000. Later, the same disease attacked his spine, and by 2006 he was wheelchair-bound. A radical course of therapy over the course of two years helped him to walk again, but not content with walking, he subsequently ran four marathons and twice climbed the forty-eight mountains over four thousand feet in his native New Hampshire. In 2016, with his guide dog Quinn, he reached the summit of Mount Kilimanjaro.

Among all these incredible achievements, however, for sheer drama nothing can compete with the moment when Pierce stood on the high platform of the King of the Swingers obstacle and reached out to locate the trapeze bar with his white stick. You reach that platform above a pool of water by climbing thirty stairs. The trapeze bar is eight feet away from the platform edge, and Mudders must leap to grab it. If they do, they then swing the full arc of the trapeze to ring a bell before dropping into the cold water below. Only about 10 per cent of Mudders catch the bar and swing far enough to ring a bell. Thinking about all those things, Randy stood on that platform and reached out for the trapeze bar with his white stick and prepared to jump.

Speaking about it now, he traces the courage to be up there at all back to something he was told a couple of weeks after blindness struck all those years ago.

When he got the news that his sight could not be saved, Randy was only a year out of college. He loved his job designing the hardware for communication products, he was heavily involved in sports, and felt as if his life was just beginning. Then just as suddenly it seemed like it had come to a full stop.

'When I went into the hospital, I was very gregarious, very exuberant,' he says. 'But it very quickly became clear that they weren't going to make me better. And somewhere in there I changed my manner and withdrew. I got bitter and angry. One day, after a couple of weeks of this, a nurse got me a day pass, and she and her husband took me out on a boat on a waterway nearby. It was Memorial Day. She said there was something she needed to tell me, but that her colleagues didn't think I was ready to hear it, which was why she had taken me out of the hospital. She said it pretty bluntly, and I'll never forget her words. She said, "Randy, you aren't the same person who came in here. When you came in here you were so full of life we all wanted to do everything possible to help you, but right now, if we were to meet you for the first time, we would not have any motivation to try to give you that extra assistance. If you could find the person you were, people are always going to want to be a part of your life. If you can't ever find that person again, you are going to lose all the support that could help you do anything you want in this world. That would be a waste because you had an awful lot of potential when you came in here."'

It was a tough thing to hear, but Randy never forgot that lesson. From that moment on he vowed never to let blindness – or bitterness about his blindness – define him. He would instead see it as a challenge and an opportunity to find new possibilities in his life. 'I felt disabled and therefore was disabled, not because of my blindness but because of my inappropriate mental response,' he says. 'It took a little bit of time for me to say "Hey, I'm the one limiting myself," but gradually I realized that if I found ways to solve problems, I could still be the man I was always meant to be.'

He realized the best argument against 'you can't do that' was always just to do it. He used karate, in bouts against sighted fighters, to improve his focus and awareness, and eventually earned a black belt. He relearned basketball and baseball and football. And then, after his spine was damaged, he relearned how to walk.

The spine injury affected Randy's balance, but he found the quicker he moved forward, the more chance he had of staying upright. He had lost all feeling below the knee, but with the help of a guide dog and a gyroscope on his tongue to help his balance, he worked out how to run by 'feeling the ground through his thighs'. And he also developed a taste for heights.

Randy's mountain-climbing experience had been crucial when he attempted Tough Mudder. He did his first event in 2014 in New England, running with a team of five friends.

One of the consequences of Randy's blindness is that he has had to get used to sometimes being helped. One of the things he loved about Tough Mudder was that he got to give plenty of help too. 'I'm six foot four and I'm strong, so when we are coming up to obstacles where people need a lift, Berlin Walls, Pyramid Scheme, I'm a great booster. I believe positive people accomplish things. I'm independent and strong willed, so taking help is something that took a while for me to accept. But now I know how I feel when I get to help somebody – I realize if I let somebody help me, I'm letting them get that good feeling too. What a gift I am giving them!'

When Randy got up the steps to the platform of King of the Swingers, there were friends around him, but this time he was very much on his own, about to leap into thin air to try to catch something he couldn't see. There is a viral video that captures the moment. 'If you look on the video you can see I use my stick so I can actually point my toes at the outer edges of the bar I have to grab hold of to keep my bearings,' he says. 'The other thing is I didn't try to grab the handlebar itself because it's small, and I don't have great sensitivity in my hands, so I aimed to hug the vertical bar above. I overjumped the thing, of course, because of the adrenaline, but I held on for dear life and started to swing.' In his head Randy had a countdown; he reckoned he needed to count two seconds to leave the bar at the optimum moment to ring the bell. But, of course, once he jumped everything speeded up and slowed down at the same time. 'As I swung,' Randy says, 'I counted and jumped and reached for the bell without knowing quite whether I had rung it before hitting the water. It was silent underwater, but as I pushed out I could hear the crowd screaming and yelling and I realized I'd done it. Nothing could wear me down after that. We ran another hour and I was still on an adrenaline high.'

Randy has carried that moment with him in the years since, and no one who has watched the film will forget it either. It proved to him that there are ways to overcome the limitations that life puts in front of you and that there are 'a million cool things to do in this world'. He and his wife have a big anniversary this year. They've never been to Niagara Falls, but Randy had heard they put a zip line across them. It's been a hard job getting people who run that wire to approve a blind person going across it, but he thinks he's winning the argument. 'I just say: before you say no, let me show you a few of the things I've done lately. After that it's quite hard for them to argue.'

CHAPTER 4
Authentic at Scale: Growing a Tribal Culture

A small team of A-plus players can run circles around a giant team of B and C players.

– Steve Jobs

The first chocolate feet arrived in the Tough Mudder office in 2012. We had grown fast, from three events in the first year to fourteen the next, and then to thirty-five. There were articles in the *Wall Street Journal* and the *Financial Times*. Suddenly everyone wanted to work for us. We needed to hire a hundred new people in 2012, but we were getting five thousand CVs a month. Some people were extremely persistent. A strange trend started in which intern hopefuls would send us giant shoes, some of them muddy from our events, with a note that said: 'Now I have my foot in the door . . .' And then somehow that evolved into people sending cast moulds of their foot made from chocolate. We got maybe half a dozen chocolate feet.

There were also bags of biscuits and homemade cakes, which the guys who worked in the warehouse would share. I felt obliged to point out a few times that this was food from strangers, sent in the mail. And that we had one or two enemies at the time. Mr Mouse was still on our case, and the rivalry with Spartan was at its height. In the end, we had to ban eating food that came with CVs.

There was a form of flattery in this phenomenon, but it also presented us with another challenge: how could we grow fast and stay true to our values? All start-up businesses stand and fall by virtue of who they hire, but I believed assembling the right core team was more crucial to us than to most. If we were to create and nurture a tribal culture, we would need to find and employ people who took it to heart. If we were serious about our pledge to Mudders, we had to live up to those values in everything we did.

It was straightforward enough to begin with. Our first recruits – alerted by ads on Craigslist – remember being grilled by Guy and me in a cupboard-sized room that doubled as a storage space in the warehouse in DUMBO. The opening questions were generally: do you have a computer? And do you have access to a car? But after that our queries became more rigorous.

One of the reasons that we were getting so many applications (and chocolate feet) was that we offered a get-out-of-jail card to people who had gone from the self-starting freedom of student life to the 360-degree micromanagement of the corporate world. Jesse Bull, who joined us after the third event, and is still with us, was typical. He was a seriously creative English literature graduate who had started out trying to make documentaries before finding himself in a job at Barclays investment bank to impress or appease his then girlfriend. After the financial crash, he ended up in the wreckage of Lehman Brothers, desperately looking for an escape route to something he could believe in.

When we interviewed Jesse, we were, happily, able to point to one possible belief system on a poster on the wall – a prototype credo that Guy and I had written, which was an attempt to translate the Mudder pledge recited at the starting line of events into a set of principles or a philosophy that we could apply to the business. We made the credo into a poster and stuck one on every wall of the office. Much of it had been adapted from the Toyota mantra of *kaizen*, or the principle of continuous improvement. Some of it was drawn from my experience at the Foreign Service. Some of it just felt about right. The ten points were these:

1. Have fun
2. Push boundaries
3. Take responsibility
4. Ask why?
5. Be honest
6. Embrace change
7. Accept only the best
8. Focus on the long term
9. Look out for each other
10. Enjoy the journey

I don't know what recruits like Jesse made of it in his interview – they were applying to work on mud runs and being presented with the ten commandments – but along with the rest of the people we hired, he was soon left in no doubt that we meant every word.

We knew that if we were to sell our values to the wider Tough Mudder tribe – those ideas of cooperation and continual self-improvement and collective energy – they had to be embodied in our people. Authenticity wasn't an aspiration for us; it had to be a reality. In an effort to reinforce our instincts at interviews, we took each new employee on for eight weeks as a paid intern before committing to a full-time contract. There were only two jobs in the first year or so: business analyst and event planner. Those eight weeks of induction were designed as a total immersion in the culture, with a series of mentoring sessions and appraisals, plenty of hands-on responsibility at events – all designed to see if there was a fit on both sides. At the end of the eight weeks there was what we called a 'cultural interview' – which led to lots of Chairman Mao jokes – designed to test how fully the intern had internalized the culture, and thus understood the values.

If that sounds cultish, I'm unapologetic. When organizations talk about creating an innovative business culture, a lot of people focus on the external symbols. The ping-pong and foosball tables in the office, the team-building Thursday beers after work, the company ski weekends and the anything-goes dress code. At TMHQ we have all those things. But they are marginal to what we are really about. A culture is built up over months and years of good practice, questioning and improvement. Of doing things the right way and having anyone who comes into the group or participates in an event recognize what that means. Culture is all the things that happen in an organization when the boss isn't looking.

Tony Hsieh describes, in his book *Delivering Happiness*, how he built his online shoe business Zappos by concentrating on service and integrity above all else. 'Your personal core values define who you are,' he argued, 'and a company's core values ultimately define the company's character and brand. For individuals, character is destiny. For organizations, culture is destiny.' I think that's true, and doubly so when you are 'delivering happiness' as an experience that asks people to take on and display some of the virtues of that culture themselves.

In this sense, we believed, in our initial phase of recruiting, that a candidate's previous career path and qualifications were less important than his or her willingness to embrace our credo. Though we had no experience of event management, the plan was never to go out and hire people from the event industry. We had obstacles where participants jump through flames and we feared the first thing an outside event person might instinctively do was pull out a fire extinguisher.

Sometime early on in our discussions about the Tough Mudder culture – in one of our many debates about who to hire – someone suggested that our criteria could be boiled down to a single phrase, borrowed from the New Zealand All Blacks rugby team: 'No Dickheads' (our equivalent of Google's 'Don't Be Evil'). Later, I had everyone read James Kerr's book *Legacy*, about his time spent with the All Blacks, studying their culture: 'In Maori, *whanau* means "extended family", Kerr observed. 'It's symbolized by the spearhead. To be effective, all its force must move in one direction. Hence the All Blacks select on character as well as talent, which means some of New Zealand's most promising players never pull on the black jersey – considered dickheads, their inclusion would be detrimental to the *whanau*.'

There were clear cases of individuals who would never be part of our Tough Mudder *whanau*. In our first year, we took on an intern who had worked for a year or two on Wall Street. On his first day, I asked him to go and look at a potential event venue and report back. Upon his return, he sat at my desk and insisted that before he gave his verdict on the venue we negotiate his terms of employment. He suggested a three-hundred-dollars-a-day retainer in addition to a salary of two hundred thousand dollars – oh, and 10 per cent of the company. I laughed for a while and terminated his internship on the spot. It didn't end there, unfortunately. For his road trip, I'd given him my Tough Mudder credit card details and, apparently in revenge, he used those details to sign up for a variety of extreme porn websites in my name, including dwarfporn.com, which for a while was a stubbornly returning charge on our credit card statements. He wouldn't have lasted long with the All Blacks.

Some other hires proved wrong in less blatant ways. We took on a marketing director who had a very impressive background in selling conferences for professionals. Our marketing was quite edgy from the outset. We wanted to contrast our irreverent, muddy approach with events like marathons or triathlons that were much more clean living and earnest. We were never short of photographs to make this point. It quickly became clear, however, that we had somehow employed a marketing director who insisted exclusively on pictures of people in box-fresh T-shirts with a perfectly blue sky behind them and who could see no merit at all in a shot of a bunch of dirty people hauling a friend bum-first over a wall.

It often proved more effective, particularly at the outset, to use people without specialist experience, but with a clear understanding of what we were about, to get a message right. Alex Patterson, hired as a lawyer, was invaluable in this respect. Before joining Tough Mudder he had quit his job as a tax attorney and considered joining the FBI, or working in human rights, or just going surfing. He was, as he describes it now, really 'best at entering the fog, not fearing failure, creating something new'.

To try to focus these start-up, fog-entering energies as the company grew and we required different kinds of expertise, I created the internal Tough Mudder University. It was great to have people who understand our no fear, no whining culture, but as we grew they also needed some specialist insights. Rather than take the risk of hiring people who had those skills but did not understand our context, I tried to use TMU to offer relevant examples of best practices in different areas of the business. I have been critical of some of the small-minded aspects of the culture of competition at Harvard, but there was no doubt that the structure of the way it taught business – using rigorously examined case studies from the real world – was an invaluable tool. At Tough Mudder I personally took on the challenge of teaching case studies in the Harvard manner to fifteen or twenty people at a time each month. This was a big commitment of time on my part when time was in quite short supply, so whatever the employee's role at Tough Mudder was, I required everyone to carefully read and prepare the cases in advance and to be prepared to discuss the implications for our business just as seriously as they might in a Harvard lecture room. I could be fairly unforgiving of those who did not put time and effort into this preparation. I tried to pick cases relevant to what was happening at the company at the time – looking at Microsoft's innovation strategy or at Starbucks and the selling of a cultural experience or Innocent smoothies and the art of storytelling.

Most often we returned to *kaizen* and Toyota. A series of awards evolved, rewarding Tough Mudder initiative and clear thinking and honesty in owning up to mistakes. We called winners Kaizen Ninjas. Given the technical and logistical challenges of delivering the increased number of events – and the resultant exponential growth in things that could go wrong – Toyota's 5 Whys principle became integral to our Kaizen Ninja approach. This was the idea that if something went wrong, you asked why five times to get at the real reason for it. So, if a rope broke at a Tough Mudder obstacle, the series of questions and answers would go something like this: why did the rope break? It was the wrong rope. Why was it the wrong rope? Because we bought the cheap rope. Why did we buy the cheap rope? Because the budget was too low. Why was the budget too low? Because we don't know how to budget properly. Why don't we know how to budget? Because we don't have that capability in obstacle design. Then you'd buy new ropes but also hire someone with the capability that was lacking or develop it in the current staff.

I thought hard, too, about ways we could incorporate these kinds of self-critical habits into our everyday practice. The way I had been allowed to work in the Foreign Service seemed to be a valuable model. My training was often quite abstract, involving role-play and continuous scrutiny to encourage resourcefulness; it impressed on me the need to have high standards of integrity, to be honest about strengths and failings. At age twenty-four, I had been given a complex and highly responsible series of problems about the structures of funding of various terrorist groups and left to work out the best way to dismantle them. Almost anything was possible within certain rules. I became frustrated at one point that I could only withdraw cash that I needed for one assignment by completing a cumbersome and time-consuming docket system. I discovered, however, that the rules allowed me to withdraw a hundred thousand pounds at a time. I bought a twenty-pound safe and some heavy-duty bolts from the local hardware store, withdrew cash up to the authorized limit, and installed the safe under my desk and employed it as required. I wanted Tough Mudder employees to be confident that they could display that kind of initiative at every level, the kind of initiative that was sometimes crucial to negotiating the obstacles in the event itself. The culture was designed both to promote supportive teamwork and also to generate a high degree of personal responsibility. People were encouraged to always look for better solutions to problems rather than accept the answers they had been given.

With this in mind, we introduced a policy of unlimited holiday. At the beginning of the year, after some discussion, everyone at TMHQ is given a set of objectives. And each person is told, 'If you can get it all done in six months, that's brilliant; you can take the rest of the year off.' The flip side of that, however, is that each person truly owns his or her objectives. If you don't believe that you are going to hit the targets, it is up to you to address that fact and to explain precisely the reasons why. The idea was a way of distributing responsibility throughout the organization, even to more junior employees – and it works. Most people see it as liberating, and adapt quickly to the expected level of responsibility. A few get freaked out by not being told what to do. And sometimes people get to take extended breaks.

Again, the practice of the event itself provides a good example of the positive intersection between teamwork and personal achievement. Whatever role people play at Tough Mudder, they are required to work at least one event a year, and ideally – though there is no compulsion – to also run in one. It's not only a way of muddily connecting everyone with what we do, it also delivers a shared fund of adventures and stories that continually reinforce Tough Mudder culture – if you witness Randy Pierce jumping for the trapeze at King of the Swingers or any of the other innumerable small acts of courage and kindness out on the Mudder course, you return to the office with a greater sense of mission. In the office after each event we circulate stories from the road and try to make sure that everyone in the company understands ways in which their contribution fits in to the bigger picture. As I say all the time, we are not curing cancer – but we are often making meaningful small differences in people's lives, and we should take pride in that fact.

We like to think these habits and this pride filters through to our tribe. We recently did some research looking at the motivations of Tough Mudders who had taken the pledge in 2015. Their most popular reasons for signing up to the challenge and coming back included 'doing something outside my comfort zone' and 'introducing others to something awesome' closely followed by 'having an epic story to tell', 'connecting with others' and 'defining success for myself'. It's interesting to note that our internal staff appraisals come up with similar motivations.

In our external research we found that hardly anyone was just there for mud and beer. They said things like, 'Something happens at Tough Mudder. It's like what happens in a natural disaster' (by which I trust they mean it develops a 'blitz spirit' rather than 'you get cold and terrified and wet'). Or they referenced the insistent 'real life' of the event: 'Social media is about the past. You're looking at things that happened. But with Tough Mudder you're doing it. You're there.' Often, almost universally, Mudders felt empowered in a way that they could take into the rest of their lives: 'There were times when I was going through the pain and I felt like I was getting shot at. It hurt! But now, it goes back to: "Oh, I can conquer the world."'

Communication of such stories is the lifeblood of the culture and the tribe – and it must go in all directions, not just from TMHQ outwards, but also from the wider Mudder tribe back into TMHQ. Just as Mudders draw strength from each other out on the course, so we can use their determination and energy to inspire the business. An important part of that is to consistently dramatize the idea of the company to our employees, particularly new arrivals. The Mudders themselves are a crucial aspect of that. Some of it comes from seeding ideas and reinforcing messages out in the wider tribe, whether by viral feeds or direct messaging or face-to-face contact at events. And some of it – perhaps the most effective part – is creating the tools to allow tribal members to share their experience of Tough Mudder and its values with their wider network. In 2012, I said in one interview that we will know when we have arrived as a brand 'when a guy goes into a bar and thinks when he tells a girl he's doing a Tough Mudder, the girl knows what he's talking about – whether the girl is impressed or not is frankly irrelevant'. Five years on I think we have reached that point – and that increasingly it will be a girl telling a guy she is doing a Tough Mudder.

More than 90 per cent of this familiarity has come through social media. When we talk about word of mouth at Tough Mudder, we mean people uploading photographs to Facebook, posting statuses about events, linking YouTube videos, Snapchatting, Instagramming, Tweeting, blogging and all the rest. We value all those channels in that they have a life and a community of their own. We spend a lot of money each year on Facebook advertising, but these platforms are amplified many times over by the network of users themselves. Social media acts as a connector of tribe members, but it means little without a shared story to tell.

That story inevitably changes a little over time. In some ways, it is relatively easy to be authentic and true to your credo when you are a 'disruptive' start-up company, with only a dozen employees. Growth comes with other challenges. Sheetal Aiyer was another of our early hires. I had known Sheetal as a friend in 2002 when he was at the US Department of Justice in Washington and I was working as an intern prior to joining the Foreign Office. He came in to help with some contract work at Tough Mudder, and ended up, like Jesse and Alex and a few others, fulfilling many key roles as we expanded. Along with Alex, Sheetal left the company last year to pursue another start-up venture; in his case, at a craft beer company in Brooklyn. I still see him often when I am in New York. He is, like all of us who have been at Tough Mudder since near the beginning, in some ways nostalgic for the excitement of growing something from nothing. It is a feeling that is hard to replicate but one that once experienced is highly addictive.

'Helping build the team and the culture for me was the most fantastic thing,' he says now. 'Because it brought together so many different people from different places. Nine times out of ten, people do not truly believe in what they are doing; they don't wake up every morning thinking they can't wait to go in to work. But at Tough Mudder in the beginning we just felt every day we were going to grow a bit personally and maybe do a bit of good in the world. I suppose that feeling is what I'm chasing again now. I think I will always be chasing it.'

I don't think – and I don't think Sheetal thinks – that that feeling has gone away from Tough Mudder, but it has inevitably evolved as we have got bigger and employed more people. In the early days of any company you tend to hire only people whom you would want to have a beer with – and all of you can fit around a bar table. As it grows you employ people who may have very different backgrounds and very different personalities but who still share those original values. The key challenge for me has been to keep that pioneering feeling alive in the organization and beyond, even as we grow. And that comes back to nurturing culture.

I'm a pretty compulsive viewer of TED talks. One that resonates with me is Joseph Pine's 'What Consumers Want'. Pine makes the case that in the past decade or so, what people have come to want above all is not commodities or luxury goods but experiences. Boutique hotels and Disneyland and drinking decent wine and listening to TED talks are all experiences. But the experiences we prize most are the ones that we consider authentic. Businesses selling experiences must above all be true to themselves, by which, Pine argues, 'they have to be what they say they are to others'. Or in other words, 'if you say you are authentic you better make damn sure you are authentic'.

Our intimacy and connection with the Tough Mudder tribe is both our strength and our early warning system. Constant two-way communication means that if we let Mudders down, in any way whatsoever, they will be extremely quick to let us know, through a variety of channels and media. One result of creating a tribal mentality is that each individual member of the tribe feels, properly, a real sense of ownership of our core values and our business. If you have something tattooed on your chest you want to make damn sure that it does not become fake or sell you out. Mudders believe in us, and like all believers they want above all not to be let down. I have been fascinated by research in how nations build allegiance from their citizens. In relatively young countries, studies show that a very strong investment in the primary or elementary school sector is invaluable – because that is the time and place where children best absorb national values. Argentina and the United States place great emphasis on allegiance to the flag, for example, in ways that many more sceptical Old World Europeans might find a little cringeworthy.

At Tough Mudder we adopted a little of that young-country mentality, with a counter-cultural twist, and have been successful in making people feel a version of that attachment – through the headband, and the pledge, the commitment of time and courage, the culture of sharing stories. If you run a 10K, it's probably not your identity; it's something you did last Saturday. Even if you finish a triathlon you are not primarily a 'triathlete'. But if you complete a Tough Mudder, you are a Tough Mudder. People make that fact the prominent descriptor on their Linkedin and Facebook profiles because it means something, both to them and to their circle – it's shorthand for a set of values, an attitude to the world. Before smartphones and tablets delivered news, people used to define themselves – in Britain at least – by which newspaper they read. They would carry it with the masthead showing to signal which tribe or class they aspired to. There are fewer such effective tribal signifiers now, but Tough Mudder is perhaps becoming one of them. Among the strangest, proudest moments I've experienced, after one of the first events, was being on the New York subway on a Monday morning and seeing a bunch of people heading to jobs in the city wearing their Tough Mudder headbands. Another time, after the first event we had run in the Midlands of England near where I grew up, I happened to park in Worksop behind a guy who had a headband hanging from his rearview mirror. It made me feel strangely emotional to see the orange band in my home town, and I had to take a photo. The guy understandably came and confronted me to ask what on earth I was doing taking a picture of his car. When I explained, he was suddenly all smiles. If we had not been English we might have hugged; as it was, we shook hands.

That kind of personal identification with the idea of the brand means we can never be complacent. As we expand, our authenticity is constantly policed by the Mudder community for signs of deviation from those founding principles. Jesse Bull is now SVP of Brand, and one of his roles is to keep up a 24/7 conversation with the Mudder community, in particular the die-hard legionnaires who have done thirty events or more and who hold us to account if the thirty-second event is not a slight improvement on the thirty-first. This core group has a full-on life of its own – Jesse's evenings and weekends rarely pass without at least a few urgent comments and questions to respond to.

Sometimes I dip into these conversations, which mostly happen in Facebook groups. It remains a curious thing to eavesdrop on Mudders talking all night about tiny changes in the company, or little tweaks we have made to obstacles or events. There are often heated debates about whether this or that thing – something that might have been changed on a whim six months earlier – represents a departure from our true spirit. Early adopters feel themselves, rightly, to be keepers of the original Tough Mudder flame.

Last year, at the last minute, we decided to put on a ticketed community event at World's Toughest Mudder in Las Vegas, at which I would give a short talk and thank-you to participants. We had space for only about a third of the fifteen hundred participants and no time to market the event. We sold the tickets, but the funny thing for me was to see the number of Facebook comments afterwards about whether it was cool or not to go to the official event or instead 'just hang out with the community'. *Hold on,* I thought, *we created the community too!*

That sense of tribes within tribes reveals the depth of belonging and ownership among Tough Mudders. One of the case studies I return to most often in our Tough Mudder University is Harley-Davidson – the archetypal example of the way in which people can gather around the authentic values of a brand and have it say something enduring about who they are. Harley-Davidson had created part of that culture by creating covetable motorcycles in a time and place where freedom became synonymous with the open road. The rest of it, however, came from the company's efforts to nurture community. It sponsored Harley owners' groups and affiliated chapters that not only organized events and rallies and weekend gatherings but also took part in some community service. There are well over a thousand of these groups across America and the world, with more than half a million members. The case study examined the ways in which over the twenty-five years since the owners' groups had started, the brand had become for many members almost a full-time way of life and a consistent worldview. When you bought a Harley, you were not just buying a motorcycle; you were buying membership in a community.

One of the most gratifying aspects of what we have done is to see some of this kind of Harley-Davidson tribal spirit being created around Tough Mudder quite quickly in real time. To observe, across cultures and continents, how the values we tried to instil in the business on those first *kaizen* posters have now been taken to heart and adopted by Mudders the world over. In my more sentimental moments, this feels to me a little like the opposite of the famous 'Stanford prison-guard experiments', beloved of psychology graduates. That experiment demonstrated that ordinary people would quickly inflict cruelty on others without question if it were modelled to them. With a few simple mechanisms – the bonding of the Tough Mudder pledge and the anthems at starting lines and the architecture of obstacles that encourage teamwork – along with seven years of commitment to a set of values, we seem to have identified a community that consistently spreads camaraderie instead.

One of the defining aspects of this community, I think, is the fact that we have always had many volunteers working at the events. We call them Mudder MVPs or Most Valuable Players. Following the example of Wikipedia, we've developed the idea that communities are more likely to form spontaneously when there is an absence in at least part of the system of a financial motivation. Volunteers represent the Mudder idea that we are all in this together. From the beginning, we wanted to incentivize sympathetic people to come and help at our events. We offer a very significant – up to 90 per cent – discount on the entry fee to run a Tough Mudder for people who volunteer for a day first. The advantage of this goes both ways – we get a motivated and engaged group of often local people on-site, strengthening our links with the community. And the volunteers have a fun day, get some swag, and get to see our values lived firsthand before they find themselves on the starting line.

The idea has proved so popular that we now have a number of MVPs at each event who turn up cheerfully at five in the morning to help without any thought of going on to run a Tough Mudder. They volunteer just because they love volunteering. Miranda and Guy Richardson, almost ever present at our UK events, are great examples of these super volunteers who have become so vital to the Tough Mudder tribe.

In her day job Miranda is an apprenticeship tutor, helping difficult students settle into their first experience of work. Her husband Guy is a self-employed gas engineer, carpenter, plumber – a handy man to have on-site. Miranda is one of the few members of the tribe who does not have the Tough Mudder pledge but the alternative volunteers' pledge tattooed on her shoulder. Her story, and her enthusiasm, is not atypical. It began for her in 2012 when Guy ran a Tough Mudder. She saw the volunteer programme and signed up for the next event. She and Guy supervised the obstacle called Trench Warfare for ten hours in a wet field – cheering people on, helping a few in difficulty. 'On the three-hour drive home, we were both just buzzing from it,' she recalls. 'And straightaway I got online and applied for the next one.'

After that they were hooked. They started getting to the site early, on Friday, to help set up, and staying late on Sunday to help pack up. Now there is quite a large network of volunteers that do every event and keep in touch online. The sense of stewardship they epitomize runs deep in the Mudder community. 'Just occasionally,' Miranda says, 'you get Mudders who don't get it. A couple of seasons ago we had a bunch of runners we called "the glee club" who seemed to want everything for nothing. They would play the "do you know who I am?" card to new Mudders, try to pull rank because they had done the event a few times. When that happened, we volunteers made it clear that nobody cared about their egos. They disappeared soon afterwards.' People tell Miranda she is crazy to give up her summer weekends putting ice into Arctic Enema or whatever. 'But,' she says, 'for me just to help get one person over a wall or into the water, one person who turns around and says "thank you, I didn't know I could do that" makes it all worthwhile.'

This kind of spirit has always been infectious throughout the Tough Mudder community, viral in the best sense of the word. A good test of its reach is that it runs all the way from our volunteers through to the elite athletes at the most 'serious' end of what we do, in the gruelling annual twenty-four-hour 'race' to be World's Toughest Mudder. We don't do superstars in our Tough Mudder world – but if we were to, it would be hard to ignore the claims of Amelia Boone, an athlete who now features regularly on the cover of *Runner's World* and who has been the women's champion at World's Toughest three times. An in-house lawyer for Apple in Silicon Valley, Amelia is among the only competitors to keep running for twenty-four hours in the desert without a rest. She keeps coming back not for the glory of 'winning' but because, she says, 'you will never find a race like World's Toughest Mudder – where you are technically running against other people but where you will still see the leader out there stopping to help people up over walls or out of the water. It is just this unwritten rule; no one questions it, that is how it is.'

Amelia studied social anthropology before she became a lawyer, with an interest in the way that social norms and gossip were used by indigenous tribes to create and maintain healthy and coherent cultures. Tough Mudder, she suggests, is the closest she has come to seeing that tribal spirit in action in the contemporary world.

'If I am out for a run and I see someone wearing a Tough Mudder headband or T-shirt, there is always a big smile and a nod of recognition between us,' she says, as if she is speaking of a pair of Yanomami natives coming across each other on a forest trail. It's a nod, she suggests, that communicates a great many things – not only shared philosophies and kinship but also the recognition that 'I may well have pushed your wet arse over a wall at some point last year.'

MUDDER LOVE: Jeremy Richman

We can – and do – talk a lot about the theory of creating a tribal culture and the ties that bind the Mudder community, but the living examples of those communities, how they meet weekly to train together and live some of our values, are always our best argument.

In 2015, we made a series of films with some inspirational Tough Mudder teams. The idea was to share some of the stories that we thought best articulated the values we tried to promote. The videos quickly went viral in the community. One team that we featured in the film *Mud for Brains* is led by Dr Jeremy Richman, who lives with his wife, Jennifer, in Newtown, Connecticut. Jeremy's team grew directly out of one of the most shocking tragedies that America has witnessed: the murder of twenty schoolchildren and six of the staff at Sandy Hook Elementary School in December 2012. Jeremy and Jennifer's daughter Avielle, then aged six, was among the children who were killed that day.

In the short film, which is one of the most affecting things I have ever watched, Jeremy and Jennifer sat and talked with enormous courage and clarity about the ways in which they had tried to go on living after they had lost their daughter. One of the first things they had done was to set up a foundation in Avielle's name to investigate the neurological causes of the kind of violence that took place at Sandy Hook and to educate communities about the findings in the hope of preventing further tragedies. Among other things the website of that foundation describes exactly what kind of child Avielle had been, and the loving family Jennifer and Jeremy had created. It begins like this:

'Our daughter, Avielle Rose Richman, was born in San Diego, California, on October 17, 2006, into a family of storytellers. With a spitfire personality, and a love of laughter, Avielle was rarely without a giant grin, and was often barefoot. Like her parents, she loved stories and demanded them as she was falling asleep, taking a bath, riding in the car, and on every walk she took. Avielle had a grand spirit of adventure. . . . When asked what she wanted to be when she grew up, Avielle would reply that she wanted to be an artist . . . and a spy . . . oh, and a fairy princess, and a writer. She also had a strong sense of justice and fairness and was a steadfast friend for anyone she thought in need. That same sense of justice and fairness could also make every negotiation quite a stressful chore for her parents. As a result, Avielle was often reminded of the family rules:

1. No whining
2. Show respect to people and things that are special
3. You get what you get and you don't pitch a fit
4. Mind your manners and social graces
5. No button pushing
6. Take responsibility for your own actions'

The Tough Mudder film showed the route that Jeremy took in his daily run through Newtown and Sandy Hook. The hardest part of that run, he said, was the part that took him past the fire station, which was where the parents from Sandy Hook had waited for information about the mass shooting at the school. On the roof of the fire station a constellation of stars has been painted: twenty small stars, one for each child, and six large stars, one for each adult.

Jeremy and his wife are both scientists. His research background is in therapeutic mechanisms for Alzheimer's disease. After Avielle died he gave up that work and concentrated all his efforts on the foundation.

'We knew we had to find a reason to keep getting out of bed in the morning,' he says now, looking back. 'To go on surviving and living. We decided to create the Avielle Foundation on two principles, which we wrote down three days after the murders. Firstly, to take a scientific approach to try to better understand this kind of violence, to fund research that looks at the risk factors that lead to it and the compassionate factors that lead away from it. And secondly, to educate people on the invisible world of the brain. To try to make brain health and brain illness much more visible.'

A lot of people said to him: 'What can you do about violence, Jeremy? It is in our blood, in our DNA.' He replied by saying that was true, but that we are also a social species. Kindness is also a part of our DNA. 'We evolve by collaborating and connecting,' he says. 'The better we are at communal living, the more humane we are and the more human we are.'

It was a friend and neighbour of Jeremy's called David Stowe who first told him about Tough Mudder. This was January 2014, a year after the murders. David talked about the whole tribe mentality of the event, the sense of togetherness, and Jeremy understood that immediately. With a few other friends they created a team, Mud for Brains, and signed up to run the nearby event at Mount Snow, in Vermont.

Mud for Brains has run every year since, raising funds for the foundation. In between times, a few of them meet for a 'fight night' exercise session in the garage studio at the back of Jeremy's house. 'In Mud for Brains I think we definitely push ourselves harder and farther because we are part of a group,' Jeremy says. 'On a Wednesday, we do a hard workout, and some wrestling on the mats. I've been a kung fu instructor and a martial artist my whole life, but on these nights I probably do three times what I think I can do, because we push each other on.'

Tough Mudder has been a help in challenging Sandy Hook to come together as a community in the aftermath of the tragedy, he suggests. 'There were twenty-three of us running in 2015; this year more than fifty. It is wicked hard, but we love it. I often think of it like a crucible in a scientific experiment: you put a bunch of different elements in that crucible, you heat them up, there is a reaction, and they all come out changed.'

Jeremy has come to believe it is important for everyone to find their own crucible. 'That could be giving a talk to a big audience or learning an instrument or whatever. But for me the physical challenge has all these benefits, and it is unbelievably good for your brain because it causes all these great chemicals to be released. Much of your life is spent worrying about what is going to happen tomorrow or dwelling on what happened in the past. Physical activity, particularly difficult physical activity, keeps you right there in the present moment.'

Doing this kind of activity in a group, he believes, multiplies those benefits. 'The group also helps you to overcome fear. You get on the Mudder course and everyone is afraid of something and it is often a different thing for each person. Me, I don't like heights, so

Walk the Plank is a problem. But then some people don't like the monkey bars, Funky Monkey, or some don't like the Electroshock, or the giant Berlin Wall. But the thing is, as soon as people see that you are anxious, then the whole team is behind you pushing you on. One person on our team, Kim, had ten goes at Everest last time, and there were a hundred people urging her on until she got there. No one would think of going to the next obstacle until everyone is over.

'And then, when you are done, that cold beer could be the worst swill in the world, but it tastes like heaven's glory because you have achieved something hard. No matter how hardcore you are, you are going to feel better for it.'

In many ways, Jeremy suggests, Tough Mudder is in this sense an expression of what his research into brain sickness and brain health reveals: 'I think the people who started the Mud for Brains team, including David and myself, share a similar philosophy about the importance of challenging yourself,' he says. 'When I point out the environmental factors that predict mental illness people kind of tick them off one by one and say, well, I'm probably fine; but the fact is that if you are not actively engaged in the protective factors then you are moving into unhealthy territory, that is a fact of life. There is no steady state. For proper mental health you have always got to be seeking improvement and growth and new connections, because that is how you stay alive and how you thrive.'

'Resilience' is a word Jeremy and his wife have heard a lot in the last few years. 'The fact is,' he says, 'I think you are as resilient as you happen to be. The reason I think I am surviving, I didn't commit suicide or give up on everything, is because of the community we have, the people around holding us up, and as far as we can, us holding them up. That's why Tough Mudder resonates.'

Jeremy and Jennifer and their second daughter, now three, often go up and spend Sundays at the graveyard where Avielle and her classmates are buried. 'The secret to community and the secret of connection is to make yourself vulnerable,' he says. 'When you have children, they don't have a sense of mortality like you do, and it is good that they don't because if they did they would never leave the house. They grow by overcoming fears. I believe it is critical throughout life to do things that scare you; you have to put yourself out there or you never change, you never grow, you never meet new people.'

He recalls a story from when he first met Jennifer and they were travelling in China. During the Cultural Revolution all the kung fu masters had been exiled and, because of Jeremy's interest in martial arts, he and Jennifer got involved in a programme to help bring some of them home. 'We were travelling with this eighty-year-old kung fu master,' he says, 'who was in crazy good shape. He invited you to punch him as hard as you wanted and he wouldn't flinch. I asked him, through the translator, you know, "What is your secret?" I thought he was going to say you must train ten hours a day. You must be serious and disciplined. What he actually said was this: "Number one, you have to sleep well. Number two, you must get together with your friends. And number three, it is very important that you laugh every day." I have never forgotten that.'

CHAPTER 5
Better Never Stops: Making Innovation Happen

I want people moving and shaking the earth and they're going to make mistakes.

– Ross Perot

Not long after we moved into our apartment in Brooklyn, Katie was reading the papers on Sunday morning. I was, as ever, making a few notes for the week ahead on my laptop. Tough Mudder was in its first phase of do-or-die expansion. Guy and I were racing around the country trying to keep events on track and all the time thinking how we could improve them. In those early days we were necessarily inventing and innovating fast.

For much of 2010 we had been kicking ideas around in the office about new obstacles we could add to the course, and that Sunday morning I was mulling over some of the possibilities.

Katie recalls how, suddenly, my face lit up as if in a eureka moment, and I turned to her.

What is it? she wondered as I sat there grinning.

I adopted my best Bond villain voice. 'I'm going to electrocute* thousands of people,' I said.

She raised an eyebrow and went back to *The New York Times*. I guess she knew by then not to be too surprised.

I believe Peter Drucker's argument that at its most basic level, a business is really two things: innovation and marketing. You create something new and you work out a way to sell it. In our case we were trying to sell both an obstacle event, and through it, an idea about community. By the end of 2010 we were beginning to get our messaging with Mudders right, speaking to the growing tribe on social media of all kinds, but we also needed a continuous supply of new things to tell them about. Innovation was never a choice for us, always a necessity. I knew that a key part of this, a crucial way to keep Mudders engaged, was to continually replace and evolve the obstacles themselves. We didn't want Tough Mudder to get harder – the challenge itself was a kind of absolute – but we did want it to get better and to stay surprising. From very early on we committed to changing around 20 per cent of the obstacles each year. Not only did we believe it was important to innovate, we knew it was crucial that we were known – and loved – for innovating. That was the thing that would ensure the Tough Mudder tribe grew and thrived.

Back in 2010, when I had my eureka moment, we had been discussing in the office the nature of childhood fears, the things your parents tell you to avoid at all costs, and how we might incorporate

---

* My extremely patient general counsel, Marc Ackerman, likes to remind me that he prefers using the term 'electrify' to 'electrocute', as the latter is defined as to 'injure or kill someone by electric shock'. Sure, it hurts, but the vast majority of injuries on the obstacle occur when Mudders fall awkwardly as they try to twist their bodies away from the electrified wires, not from the shock itself.

some of them in the Tough Mudder challenge. The combination of electricity and water was high up that list. What if we delivered a jolt of electricity to our Tough Mudders? And what if we made it the last obstacle, the one they had nagging in the back of their minds all the way round the twelve miles?

The impulse behind this wasn't sadistic (at least, I tell myself, not completely). We wanted as many challenges as possible in a Tough Mudder that you couldn't prepare for physically and which were above all a test of mental fortitude, of courage.

We call these obstacles 'primal fear challenges'. They are not like, say, the monkey bars of Funky Monkey, where, should your grip give out, you just drop into muddy water. Electroshock Therapy's live wires tap into a real psychological anxiety. We toyed with a few other possibilities – spiders, snakes, but rejected them as too contrived (not to mention the animal welfare considerations and the logistics of transporting two hundred live tarantulas to each event). We briefly tried an obstacle that involved people drinking hot pepper sauce but abandoned it. For one thing, it felt too much like a gimmick (we hate gimmicks!) and for another it caused most people at TMHQ to vomit. Anyhow, we kept brainstorming about a hook that was not an athletic achievement or test of stamina but an authentic test of grit. And we kept coming back to electricity. Who is not anxious in the presence of a live wire?

As we had learned with other obstacles, there was no manual for how to create these kinds of challenges. You can't go to a website to figure out how to regulate several thousand people navigating monkey bars over a water pit or sliding feet first into an ice bath. Trying to turn Electroshock Therapy into reality, we searched hard for reliable research about delivering electric shocks to people in large numbers. Google the idea and you quickly ended up in some of the Internet's darker corners. So we decided to set up a prototype. The only true test was for us to build it, put ourselves through it, and keep modifying it until we were sure it was predictably safe and it worked. If we were confident of running through EST hundreds of times, then we could, hand on heart, let Tough Mudders try it too.

But how in the first place to construct such a thing? Should we call an electrician from the Yellow Pages? If in doubt, my first thought was often Nolan.

Nolan Kombol had joined Tough Mudder almost accidentally. He was an outdoors nut who happened to be working for the climbing magazine that had occupied the first office space we rented. That magazine was in the process of relocating when we arrived and Nolan gravitated to us. He helped with the early events, full of ideas and stamina, and I persuaded him to join us full time. On something of a whim I initially made him head of sponsorship sales – as well as event logistics – and gave him what might charitably be called a 'stretch target' of a million dollars of revenue in the first year.

To his credit, Nolan didn't laugh. I did, though. I would hear him trying to cold-call the marketing director of Ford or the relationships vice president of Coca-Cola. 'Hello, my name is Nolan Kombol. I work for a company called Tough Mudder . . . Yes . . . Tough Mudder. Can I spell that? *T* for *tractor*, *O* for *octopus* . . .' He didn't get very near his target.

Nolan was much more useful at events though. He grew up on a farm near a town called Enumclaw in Washington State, and as a result he instinctively knew all sorts of practical things about construction and mud and the challenges they pose that we who had not grown up on a farm near Enumclaw in Washington State did not. As a climber, he loved solving tough puzzles and was an instinctive collaborator. When we started to talk about electricity, Nolan chipped in with his experience of the electric fences that were used to corral horses and cattle. He had been shocked many times by these fences as a kid, and though he remembered those shocks quite clearly, he had obviously survived them. That seemed as good a starting point as any.

So we constructed the first Electroshock Therapy in the office out of modified cattle fence wires and took turns at running through the hanging wires wet through, some live with ten thousand volts – about half a Taser's worth. We experimented with different densities of wires and length of run – in the end we figured it should be about a fifty-foot run over mud and hay bales, with about a thousand hanging wires to get through. The experience was unnerving, sometimes very unpleasant, but certainly survivable. It also led to another innovation for us: we decided it would be a one-time only experience. Our returning legionnaires would be spared from doing it again if they chose to. Another good reason to come back.

One of the useful things about launching such an obstacle in the United States is that health and safety regulations are comparatively light. (By the time we came to launch in Australia and the United Kingdom, where the opposite is the case, we had a year's worth of safety data, but even so we needed to provide a full medical analysis, signed by a doctor who asserted that the obstacle 'was no more dangerous than a cow fence', which was either reassuring or not, depending on your feelings about cow fences.)

Despite this, it was with more than usual paternal concern that I watched the first Mudders negotiate Electroshock Therapy at our opening event of 2010 at Tri-State, in Arizona. I have a pragmatic frame of mind. I believe in trusting the data. Everyone had assured me that Electroshock Therapy would work. We had reviewed what science we could a thousand times and tested the technology over and over on ourselves. Even so, you would have to be extremely cool, or worse, not to have a certain amount of anxiety the night before you electrified five thousand strangers in a muddy ditch. I had long learned that the comforting cliché 'what's the worst that can happen?' was not much use when it came to thinking about Tough Mudder at three a.m. There was, after all, quite a lot of downside to our being wrong.

Now, 2.5 million people have run through those wires – a cumulative 250 billion volts delivered. It feels a little strange. Some people may imagine I take a sick pride in knowing so many people have paid us to suffer, but I mostly think about the connections and the communality of the experience that EST created.

Electroshock Therapy quickly became our most angsty obstacle because it was the hardest to imagine. We sit in focus group sessions where individual Tough Mudders say both, 'I hate it' and 'You can't change it.' Skill, strength and dexterity don't help you much because the wires are too closely arranged, so it's the obstacle that is most likely to reduce alpha men and women, those whose bodies are sculpted temples, to knock-kneed kids. There is an element of randomness to it that adds to the anxiety – it zaps a few people off their feet, others pass through unscathed. I honestly don't know how much of that is physiological or psychological, dumb luck or bravado. What I do know is that the sheer number of finishing-line conversations that begin with how much Electroshock Therapy sucked – and the shared moment that creates – must now be in the millions, if not tens of millions. That fact genuinely makes me smile, just like I did to Katie that Sunday morning when I first decided we had to include it.

Each of the obstacles we have created has something of the same emotional attachment. They are all the result of a greater or lesser amount of blood, sweat and tears, and each one has taken on a vivid personality for us. We have grown up with them, but we've also never been afraid to try to improve them. Often small modifications make all the difference. At one point we gave Everest – the signature half-pipe Mudders attempt to scale – a rounded top rather than a sharp lip, a small change that significantly increases the teamwork element because there is nothing to grab onto except other people's hands. Likewise, by listening to participants and watching dozens of events, we added a slide to Arctic Enema, which deposits you into the Dumpster of seventy-five thousand pounds of ice. Nolan described the change as a way of 'extending a *Holy shit!* moment as long as possible', which pretty well describes a lot of what we try to do.

By necessity to begin with, we did most of our innovating on-site at events. The challenge then, and the challenge now, is to keep that sense of playful possibility in how we approach things. Much has been written about the value of quick improvisation and testing in product design. Eric Ries made the 'build–measure–learn feedback loop' of 'continuous innovation' the core of his powerful Lean Startup model. The idea was to spend less time and money planning and learn by doing and quickly evaluating. We were, like any start-up, testing and learning all sorts of things all the time – systems, logistics, revenue streams and concepts. One of the great advantages we had in creating those habits was that build–measure–learn was in our DNA from creating obstacles.

For example, in the process of creating and evolving King of the Swingers, in which Mudders jump for a trapeze bar and swing out to ring a bell before plunging from a height of sixty-five feet into water, we experimented with at least a dozen versions – higher and lower platforms, bigger and smaller jumps, different kinds of trapezes – before we got the spectacular drama and Mudder experience we wanted. The sense that improvement is possible and welcome at any time tends to get squeezed out of companies or strangled by rules that remove the element of chance or last-minute spontaneity. I was determined as we grew that those habits would never form at Tough Mudder.

This was an attitude of mind. I knew from the beginning that while we had to be as efficient and have as much attention to detail as we possibly could, we also had to remind ourselves in everything we did of the experience we were delivering to people. A good part of that experience was childlike freedom in the feeling of slithering around in mud for the hell of it. Even today there can't be many children who have not on one Saturday or another set up an obstacle course and realized that the building of it was as much fun as the clambering round it. The entire goal of Tough Mudder is to revive that feeling in adults who spend half their lives sitting in a grey-carpeted cubicle staring at a screen, or stuck in traffic, or who measure their weekdays in back-to-back meetings and PowerPoint presentations. It was imperative that every time they came to a Tough Mudder – and we want the tribe to return over and over – they would be excited by a new dramatic test of character or determination or teamwork. Standing still was not an option for them and it was not an option for us.

There is a good deal of recent research to suggest that human beings are at their most creative and ingenious at about the age of eight. After that, after they get educated and told not to make mistakes and that there is only one right answer, it is often all downhill as far as creative thinking is concerned.

I can vouch for this research myself. At eight, I went on a school geography trip to a farm. Afterwards the teacher asked, 'Who is good at writing stories?' And all my friends chirped, 'William Dean! He's the best at writing stories!' So this teacher said to me: 'OK, William, you are going to write up the geography field trip for the school newspaper.' So I wrote what seemed to me like the best story I – or perhaps anyone else – had ever written: full of drama and adventure and monsters and near-death experiences and dream sequences and possibly alien abduction. When I handed it proudly to my teacher he scanned through it and said: 'What's this? William, you were just supposed to write about what happened at the farm!' I looked at him like he was crazy. 'But what happened at the farm wasn't a very good story, sir.'

Peter Skillman's Marshmallow Challenge is a good demonstration of that childlike capacity for creativity. Skillman was head of design for Palm – a company that itself benefited from the original try-and-fail prototypes of others, including Apple, to create the first handheld smartphone in 1996. Skillman's challenge was a seemingly simple one. Teams of four or five people are given twenty strands of dry spaghetti, a roll of tape, a ball of string and a marshmallow. The idea is to construct the tallest possible structure using only these items to support the marshmallow. Each team has 19 minutes to complete the task. Skillman has run the challenge with groups of all kinds. What he consistently found was this: those who generally performed best, who created the tallest towers, were recent graduates of kindergarten. And those who performed worst, whose towers collapsed or failed or didn't get off the ground? Recent MBA graduates.

There is, as Skillman argued, a good reason for this. There are two fundamental approaches to building the tower. The schoolkids tend to adopt the first one – they dive straight into construction and get the marshmallow on top of their makeshift towers right away to see what will work. Once they are involved in the building they tend to collaborate easily, focused on modifying and testing and changing, pooling ideas until they find solutions.

The MBAs tended to approach the task from the other end of the telescope. They generally had trouble to begin with deciding who in the group has the most expertise in tower construction, dredging up evidence of successful construction projects from their CVs. They then tended to spend too long deciding whose prototype tower would work and sketching blueprints. Some did calculations. By the seventeenth minute they had typically constructed a tower to their guidelines, but so far they had not put a marshmallow on top of it. Invariably, when they did, the tower collapsed and there was no time to start again.

We stuck to the eight-year-olds' way of doing things as long as we could, partly out of necessity at Tough Mudder events, working on the basis that creativity is always a dream with a deadline. Mostly the deadlines were a few days or a few hours when we were constructing and revising the first Mudder obstacles. After about event three, we knew that if we were to achieve any consistency and embed the innovation process in the team we had to bring construction in house. We hired a no-nonsense small-scale builder based in Pennsylvania. Typically, the builder and Nolan and I would stand in a field looking at an obstacle once it was in place, making changes. I would say that it needed to have two feet added here or to cut that bit off. Nolan would translate my British English into Pennsylvania builders' language. Nothing at all was ever drawn up or written down. There were some frustrations with that. But there was also a kind of built-in creative confidence.

When we started running multiple events, that trial-and-error process was too haphazard and exhausting. Nolan and I couldn't look at every obstacle we built, so we tried to formalize it a bit, without losing the make-it-up spirit. I think innovation invariably begins with design rather than abstract thinking. With this in mind we worked with a company called IDEO – slogan: 'fail often to succeed sooner' – led by the professional innovator and Haas School of Business professor Tom Kelley.

Kelley, who had grown IDEO quickly from twenty employees to five hundred, had done a lot of research into the ways that teams become creative. He argued among other things that 'great groups are more optimistic than realistic. They believe they can do what no one else has done before.'

That idea is at the heart of what Tough Mudder is about, both as a company and as a challenge. We've all seen the effects of pessimism in groups we've worked with, the people who think they are being most helpful by saying what is not possible, by pointing out the downsides before you have begun. I'm all for healthy scepticism, but when that frame of mind dominates any balancing sense of madcap hope, not much new gets achieved. A diehard realist could never start a business or navigate a Tough Mudder course.

Kelley also argued that the single inspired idea, the magic bullet that would solve everything, was not only never going to happen, it was not desirable. The journey to solutions creates solutions. You can't force creative answers. So many of the things that defined Tough Mudder, the pledge, the headband, several of the obstacles, were envisaged when we weren't consciously solving a problem. Sometimes the strain to 'be creative' gets in the way; allow yourself some space to kick back and often you find the answer arrives. There has to be a balance between structured problem solving and space for improvisation and we worked hard to incorporate that principle in the way we designed obstacles.

Ingrained knowledge of structure leads intuitively to creativity. Everyone loves the idea of the one-off genius who comes up with the killer formula out of thin air. Paul McCartney may have woken up with the melody for 'Yesterday' in his head – and spent several days obsessively searching and asking where he might have heard it before – but he did so only because he had spent the previous ten years always trying and often failing nearly every day to write brilliant melodies. The theory of general relativity may have come to Einstein in a flash of frenzied understanding, but only after he had learned every hard lesson imaginable about the possible relations of space and time and let himself be open to optimistic possibility. Creativity is always a learned habit, as well as a rush of blood. 'The key,' Tom Kelley argued, and this obviously resonated a lot with us, 'is to be quick and dirty – exploring a range of ideas without becoming too invested in only one.' It was about always being restless for the 'Goldilocks moment', what instinctively feels just right, using that 'human ability to be intuitive, to recognize patterns, and to construct ideas that are emotionally meaningful as well as functional'.

As they grow, businesses tend to be fearful of processes that cannot be simply broken down into their constituent elements. For this reason they tend to be most fearful of all about innovation: why divert resources from what you know for a fact works to something that no one has tried before? The simple answer to that argument is that there is never in life or in business a steady state. Change is the only constant.

I was mindful, when I tried to establish some consistency in our innovation strategy, of the story of Microsoft's 'lost decade'. The tech giant was born in the spirit of exuberant creativity that saw Bill Gates and his start-up team revolutionize personal computing in a few short years. But after a decade of stellar growth the company had, by 2000, become much more cautious. Internal bureaucracy stifled the innovative energy that originally made Windows, allowing upstarts like Google, Apple and Facebook to steal all Microsoft's cool. Infamously, Microsoft marginalized teams that were pioneering prototype e-books and smartphone technology, because its accounting systems and management structure favoured optimizing existing products over creating new ones. You could say, given Microsoft's profits, that the oversight was not consequential, but that would be to overlook the fact that these game-changing advances were gifted to its rivals. Tough Mudder was, of course, working at a very different scale and in a different arena from Microsoft, but the lessons were relevant.

In contrast to that experience I kept in mind the strategy of another behemoth, General Motors, in its launch of the OnStar technology that provides in-car security, navigation and emergency services to more than six million subscribers.

General Motors was used to patterns of innovation based on the life cycle of cars: things changed slowly and were subject to endless layers of market testing and internal checks and balances before a model was launched. When the opportunity arose to seize some initiative in the fast-emerging market for networked security the company could have used the same processes – and been beaten to market by nimbler competitors.

In fact, GM leadership recognized that a different model was necessary. Against much internal opposition all normal protocols for innovation and market testing were bypassed. Chet Huber, a former military strategist brought in to run OnStar, later lectured about its 'disruptive' success at Harvard. 'My suggestion early on was that unless we could suspend those GM rules, then we shouldn't even bother with the business, because we'd end up selling eight-track tapes when everyone else was selling CDs,' he said. GM's leadership team took note of his suggestion, allowing OnStar to operate as a separate subsidiary within the company. 'Had the CEO not been willing to play interference in OnStar's early years, it never would have succeeded,' Huber argues. He developed this as a lesson: 'If you try to do something profoundly disruptive within a company, the core business will probably smother it unless the CEO purposefully ensures otherwise.'

The point is, in any company, large or small, innovation must play by different rules from the rest of the business. In these terms, Tough Mudder had to be more OnStar than Microsoft. There is always a habit among the more cautious voices in leadership teams to try to bring in controls and extra bureaucracy if a creative department takes a risk and makes a mistake, or if a new product fails. I see it as my primary job to counter those voices. Instead of attempting to stop these kinds of mistakes happening, we have tried to evolve a culture at Tough Mudder in which innovators – by which I hope I mean most of us – take responsibility for why things went wrong but are never fearful of learning and trying again.

Whether you are building a smartphone or a Tough Mudder obstacle, no prototype ever works the first time. Still, I am constantly amazed how quickly some members of our teams can write off ideas at the first sign of failure. For example, most (if not all) of my management team wanted to kill off our Urban Mudder (now called 'TM5K') concept – a free-running version of the event in city streets – because the first time we put one on it came in over budget. They couldn't see the potential; they just looked at the numbers in front of them. I mentioned that when Disneyland opened in the 1950s many things didn't work. Walt Disney had to repeatedly defend his Magic Kingdom to his executives, insist that they give it time, and learn from the parts that weren't working. TM5K returned, successfully – and with budgetary lessons learned – in 2017.

I have often been struck by how people who have been high achievers academically have a disproportionate fear of failure and how this can make them overly inclined to fall back on tried and trusted procedures and products. A lot of these people rise to leadership positions by arguing against risk. We all want to believe we have a degree of control over our lives but some of the overachievers I observed, for example, at Harvard, wanted to take this to extremes. They believed business was about leaving nothing at all to chance. I think again there is a lesson here in Tough Mudder itself. Part of committing to the event is understanding that to enjoy it you accept that you are not completely in control. You can approach it with purpose but you also have to let it come at you.

Earlier, I argued that I never had the sense at Harvard that most of the faculty understood the frame of mind required to create something from nothing. By definition, business schools mostly teach what has worked in the past. That kind of thinking can set itself against genuine innovation. It is essential in any business to have conservative voices that test new ideas against existing models. And as a business grows, it is also obviously necessary to try to put a lot of your efforts into optimizing what you do well. But that can never be your sole priority.

In a business like Tough Mudder, where people expect the energy and novelty they experienced first time around to be exceeded on each subsequent engagement with the company, I think it is my role to make sure that those optimizing voices are balanced with more disruptive ones (quite often my own). I am lucky to have a CFO, Don Baxter, who rightly puts the optimization case eloquently. Often Don's good sense prevails. But 95 per cent of my creative and productive arguments with Don start with his insistence that new concepts be made to work inside existing frameworks and my feeling that we should sometimes rip up those frameworks and start again. Those arguments are always instructive, and they lend rigour to the process of change.

Innovation must always be about creating a balance of voices that does not drown out risk. There are, of course, many more ways of putting people together than there are team-building ideas. Tom Kelley's research offers a useful list of personality types that are necessary for productive innovation. He divides these qualities into three groups: the 'learning personas' (including such types as 'the anthropologist' who is constantly venturing out to interact with other groups), the 'organizing personas' (including 'the hurdler', a 'tireless problem solver who gets a charge out of solving something that has never been done before'), and the 'building personas' (including 'the storyteller', who 'captures our imagination with compelling narratives of initiative, hard work and innovation').

I think personalities are contextual rather than fixed – we behave differently in different situations. In applying Kelley's model to our innovation team, I viewed it, like all models, less as a how-to guide than a useful tool. In small teams, it is essential that people can adopt different roles in different situations – and also that team members are capable of recognizing that fact without getting too confused about the seemingly schizophrenic behaviour their colleagues are displaying.

Putting some of that spirit into practice – and remaining mindful that you learn through experience, not theory – we engaged Tom Kelley and IDEO to work with us back in 2011. The aim wasn't just to have them come up with some ideas but also for us to get an insight into their processes and way of thinking. It was a great success. Though it didn't necessarily lead to specific new obstacles, the IDEO design studio, in which everyone was invited to make things cheaply rather than discuss them in theory, became the model for our own Innovation Lab in Pennsylvania.

The Lab – run by Nolan Kombol – is a warehouse space and a field in the glorious upstate countryside where we build and test obstacles. The site is on a farm owned by the Policelli family, the construction firm that not only creates our obstacles but is also closely involved in research and development. Duane Policelli, who with his family came to work with us full time in 2012, has the perfect CV for Tough Mudder construction. He not only has a degree in engineering and five decades of experience in major construction projects, but he also grew up on this farm. He and his two brothers, third-generation Italian-Americans, helped their father build the farmhouse on this land and then employed their construction skills in more experimental teenage projects. They built all manner of tree houses – some thirty feet up – rope swings, tunnels, a working paddleboat, a submarine from fifty oil drums that – probably fortunately – were never successfully launched. They dammed the river (and inadvertently caused the neighbouring farmer to airlift his cattle to safety); they experimented with all kinds of explosives and detonators (more scientifically in later life, once Duane had achieved his blasting licence). Duane brings all this experience to bear in the ongoing challenge of creating new obstacles.

In this sense, the Lab makes what we do in Pennsylvania sound somewhat more scientific than it is. The closest we have got to men in white coats and safety goggles was probably our experiments with homemade tear gas to create our recent Cry Baby challenge. ('It is,' as one of our 'trialists' pointed out, 'not often in life that you allow someone to spray you directly in the eyes with a random bottle of fluid. It is even less often that you would let that happen when the person holding the bottle is wearing rubber gloves and a mask.') There's no typical day for Nolan's innovation team or for Duane's construction unit. Half of the time they are travelling around the country reviewing the course designs, interacting with participants, and liaising with the course constructors on the ground. A lot of the rest of the time in Pennsylvania is spent working out the best possible way of squeezing between two barrels or running hard at a wall or putting your hands in an ice bucket. We approach these questions with proper rigour and suitable childlike enthusiasm. Each obstacle that makes it to a World's Toughest Mudder and then to a Tough Mudder will have been through five stages of structured examination and filtering. The first stage is 'ideation', which is the concept-generating part, perhaps the hardest stage of all; the general idea is that everyone should bring something new to the table, and at this stage we try to leave judgement of the merits of those new things aside. Once we have all the ideas we can muster, a quick filtering process (stage two) discards those we as a group immediately see overwhelming problems with, whether in terms of logistics, cost, safety or general disgust.

Stage three starts in earnest after we have left those possibilities on the cutting-room floor and involves quickly building mock-ups of how the obstacles might look. We know from experience that it is crucial to think in concrete rather than abstract terms when innovating. Things that sound brilliant in theory often don't add up to much in practice. Sometimes we use a 3-D printer to do this modelling, and other times we use materials on hand in Duane's timberyard and workshop. From this process, each year, we aim to have ten working models from which five will become a reality on the Tough Mudder course. Duane and his team construct these obstacles to scale, ready for testing.

Stage four of our process is what we call alpha testing. This involves Tough Mudder employees from all parts of the business spending a couple days at the Lab to put the obstacles through their paces and give a sense of what excites them and what doesn't. Nolan watches out for those obstacles that in practice best promote teamwork and those that create the most exclamatory enthusiasm; what we want to hear is, 'We have just got to have that one!' A couple of the obstacles that produce none of these responses will be discarded, before beta testing by invited Mudder participants. The five best-performing obstacles will then form that year's Tough Mudder innovations, though the process is never complete. The ongoing 'anthropological' stage is to watch carefully how the obstacles cope with volumes of people and constantly reevaluate and modify.

I like to think we are only ever as good as the obstacles we reject.

Thomas Edison once said, 'There is no such thing as failure, only ten thousand ideas that didn't work.' Some obstacles are given up more reluctantly than others. Nolan keeps a file marked 'crazy obstacle ideas'. It includes the following, mostly rejected before alpha testing:

- Spider Box: clear box crawl, with spiders, snakes and scorpions on top
- Dutch Oven: low crawl through a pungent stink box; try to get through without vomiting
- Flying Squirrel: leap between two elevated platforms, with a large fan/net in the gap; must lay out like Superman in order to clear the gap, a pike jump will cause you to fall into the net
- Stormin' Norman: charge towards a wall with tennis ball/paintball turrets aimed and shooting at you, the goal being to get through the 164-foot-long field without getting pegged and to navigate the low walls in which participants can hide along the way
- Don't Go Chasin' Waterfalls: reverse slip and slide, with a timed cascade of water dumped from the top every thirty seconds, race to the top without getting washed out
- Buried Alive: underground crawl/pit maze, through which you navigate in the pitch black; if you come out the wrong exit, you may get zapped
- Human Conductor: act as the human conduit between two live wires; make the connection to make a sound and light signal before you can proceed (uses same current as EST)
- Acid Rain: run through a container full of floating acid bubbles

Nolan has a rule of thumb. If he, as a reasonably athletic thirty-year-old male, can't successfully negotiate a new obstacle 50 per cent of the time, it is too challenging; if he can do it more often than that it is probably too easy. If he vomits, it's a sign to start again, do things differently. If he just about gets through it and wants to go back for more, it might be ready for the next stage of testing.

Quite often these days, I talk to young entrepreneurs in various forums, and the most frequent question I am asked is: how do you create a culture of innovation? My answer to that question takes in some of the experience of the Lab. That trial is often about error. I tell the young entrepreneurs that if you're not making mistakes, there are only two possible outcomes. Neither of them is good. The first possibility is that you *are* making mistakes and hiding them or are oblivious to them – and that's a big problem. The other possibility is that you are not pushing yourself to change and improve – which will quickly become a big problem down the line. Punishing honest mistakes kills creativity.

Mistakes are not an end in themselves, obviously, but unless you are risking enough to make them, you will never succeed. That risk can take many forms. Sometimes it is about the courage to challenge conventional wisdom. When I was working in counter-terrorism there was a tendency among the highly educated strategists of the Foreign and Commonwealth Office to assume that jihadists thought along the same sophisticated strategic lines as they did. It was a classic case of a highly networked and hierarchical organization confronting a loose and improvisational one. My most successful contributions involved going out on a limb to try to dismantle those preconceptions, to always try to go back to first principles and 'Think different', as Steve Jobs suggested.

Another of the things I see quite often from supposedly creative people or teams is the belief that focus groups will give them the right answer. I commission more market research than anyone at Tough Mudder, but I always do so in the knowledge that it will only give you one aspect of the solution and may well be biased against radical change: people like what they know. As Henry Ford famously said, 'If I'd asked people what they wanted they would have said faster horses.'

If you want to be radical, by definition you have to be doing something different.

There are people who argue that you can't have too big a diversity of opinions in the room for new thinking to emerge. I'm not sure that is true either. Polarized disagreement isn't creativity. While it is crucial to tolerate plenty of possibility, there also has to be the prerogative of decision making. Not every idea has to be tested. Quite often it should be enough to say something won't work – hence our second quick-rejection stage. A test version of every obstacle idea we have will cost ten thousand dollars, and I am not spending that to confirm what I know from instinct and experience.

The best quick filter we have is to constantly test new ideas against Tough Mudder values. We want our obstacle innovation to be exciting, talk-worthy and visual. Something that involves teamwork is better than something that doesn't. And after that the crucial thing is this: never become too attached to your best ideas.

One of the pieces of obstacle innovation that I am proudest of is Block Ness Monster, which we rolled out in 2016 and which has quickly become a Mudder favourite. The obstacle was originally called Twinkle Toes, had gone through all our processes – and we loved it. It was a series of pivoting balance beams semi-submerged in water designed for two people to cross together without falling in. When we installed Twinkle Toes, it received a lukewarm response: fun but nothing special. We looked at it again. The part that people enjoyed was not trying to navigate the beam in tandem but the difficulty they had in trying to get back on it once they had fallen in. That required real coordination and effort. We turned the idea inside out; we started the Mudders in the water and had them try to clamber over the rotating blocks. It turned out when you had a volume of people this could be achieved only through serious collaboration. Lots of bum pushing and hand holding and shouting and screaming. We now call Block Ness Monster our penicillin because we discovered it as if by accident.

The other thing it reminded us of was that the innovation process itself was a story worth telling. We turned a camera on Block Ness and charted the good luck of its development. Tough Mudder as an event is designed to promote ingenuity and to develop problem solving. The mini documentary series we have on the website that shows us demonstrating our own problem-solving efforts has proved extremely popular. It also helps to reinforce the ingenuity of Nolan's Innovation Lab. We used to shout a lot about how we had the best obstacles; the Lab proves it. You never have to ask whether James Bond has the best gadgets; it's enough to know he has Q. Once you have seen Q in action the question becomes unnecessary.

Innovation is catching. It is also, crucially, not confined to products. The real answer to that notion of 'fostering innovation' is that it must be fundamental to everything you do, not only at the micro level but also at the macro level; 'innovation' is really another word for growth.

Sometimes that involves – as Tough Mudder requires – deliberately taking yourself beyond your comfort zone. When we started the company, we knew that we should not hesitate to expand to Britain and Australia. At Harvard we called it the 'commonwealth strategy'. The idea was to enter countries that are similar to America and produce our events remotely.

I was insistent that we went to Germany, too, because I knew it would force the company to push its own boundaries. We could not sit back and say, 'Hey, let's use our English-speaking North American marketing department for expansion.' We would need to develop new capabilities. The lessons learned from this evolution would make it easier for us to enter Japan and other less-familiar markets. It would build resourcefulness in our teams, and give us different frames of reference.

In the past couple of years at our internal Tough Mudder University I've been teaching a couple of case studies with this deliberate stretching of boundaries in mind. One of them is Marvel Comics. There was a point in the 1980s at which Marvel appeared to have plateaued as a business. It was the most successful superhero comics company in the world. But that initial phase of creativity and growth on which the business had been built had stalled. There were only so many superhero comics that you could sell – keep adding more and you would create something like hero fatigue.

Marvel recognized this and adopted a new strategy. They didn't relinquish their core competency, which was in heroic storytelling, but instead they concentrated on developing many more channels – films, games, books, multimedia and so forth – through which stories could be told and sold. Thus they transformed themselves from being a comic book company into a global media company, all strands of which connected directly back to the authentic core of what they were first good at. New channels brought a constant stream of new fans in. Marvel did not dilute their brand by expanding; they deepened and strengthened it.

Having established Tough Mudder as an idea and an event that Mudders love, our next challenge – there is always a next challenge – has been similarly to multiply the ways that the Mudder challenge can be experienced, new ways in which people can connect with us and each other. I call these channels touch points. We have launched several variations on the original Tough Mudder theme: Mudderella, our women-only event; TM5K, the streetwise version (that I still believe will become a big success); Mini Mudder for kids; and Mudder Half, which offers an entry-level challenge. It's at the other end of the spectrum from World's Toughest Mudder, but still an authentic test of grit and courage. This last year we have built further on those formats, rolling out Toughest Mudder, an overnight challenge run on a normal Mudder weekend, and Tougher Mudder, each with its own level of difficulty and exclusive obstacles. The family of events offers a way for many more people to experience what we do, without compromising the core offering.

We have also long been thinking about creating a series of Tough Mudder studio gyms. I sometimes like to think of Tough Mudder itself as a kind of modern pilgrimage, something you prepare for and then eventually commit to with like-minded devotees once or twice a year. In that sense the Tough Mudder Bootcamp will be our church, a weekly habit, a place to hang out as well as work out, offering functional fitness and Tough Mudder camaraderie.

In the spirit of build–measure–learn, we had some fun last year constructing a cool prototype of this Bootcamp space on one floor of TMHQ, as a showcase for franchisees. The other case study I've been teaching is the Apple Store model, which shows the value of creating spaces that are both showroom and sales channel, working models of our values. Six months on, the first gym franchises are already in operation.

As a company grows and matures it can be tempting to think that your creative, learning years are behind you. Tempting, but also fatal. I was struck by the recent research that said the most reliable way to enjoy a long retirement is in fact to never retire, but to keep mastering new skills and engaging in new pursuits. (Our question to Tough Mudders at the starting line, 'When did you last do something for the first time?' should never go away.) There is a psychological condition we all succumb to called 'The End of History Fallacy'. When people are asked these two questions, 'How much have you changed in the last decade?' and 'How much will you change in the next decade?', the answers are extraordinarily consistent across all ages and groups. People believe that in the recent past they have gone through a great deal of change, but when they look to the future they believe there will be a lot less. At whatever point we are in our lives we tend to regard the present as a watershed moment at which we have finally become the person we will always be.

This is a fundamental mistake. We should never simply content ourselves with the familiar. As any Tough Mudder will tell you, completing the challenge ahead depends above all on determined forward motion, and an ability to keep adapting and trying new approaches. Likewise in the business, in any business, standing still and admiring achievements is never an option. If you are not growing, chances are you are dying.

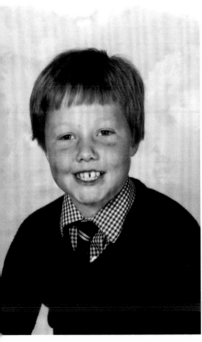

School portrait, aged eight.

Tough Mudder's first headquarters, 2015, in the DUMBO neighbourhood of Brooklyn, New York.

The Tough Mudder team, 2010. Back row (*left to right*): Will Dean, Nolan Kombol, Hunter Manchak, Alex Patterson, Guy Livingstone. Front row (*left to right*): Ashley Ellefson, Sophie Pollitt-Cohen.

Explaining the rules of *kabaddi* at Harvard Business School, 2008.

The start of the first Tough Mudder event in Allentown, Pennsylvania, 2010.

MC Sean Corvelle pumps up the crowd at the starting line.

Mudders help one another through Mud Mile.

Sixty feet of slick, rotating barriers encourage teamwork at Block Ness Monster.

Mudders 'run' through 10,000 volts of electricity at Electroshock Therapy.

Mud for Brains, Jeremy Richman's team to support the Avielle Foundation, celebrates after completing Tough Mudder New England.

Testing a prototype of Ring of Fire at the Obstacle Lab, 2014.

Noah Galloway, Tough Mudder legend and Army veteran, runs up Everest 2.0.

A Mudder is proudly crowned with an orange finisher headband at the end of a Tough Mudder.

Joining a group of more than 10,000 people who have had the Tough Mudder logo tattooed on them, a 2016 World's Toughest Mudder participant commemorates his achievement.

A legionnaire displays his badges of honour.

Running with the Tough Mudder flag in Dubai just before Tough Mudder's first event in the Middle East, 2016.

A proud moment. Being appointed a member of the Most Excellent Order of the British Empire (MBE) by Queen Elizabeth II during an investiture ceremony at Buckingham Palace, 2017.

Thousands of Mudders wait anxiously at the starting line of the 2016 World's Toughest Mudder.

The sun sets on World's Toughest Mudder, as participants swing across Kong and continue into the night.

Inside the first Tough Mudder Bootcamp, Brooklyn, New York, 2017.

A Mudder crosses Funky Monkey while dangling over a pit of mud and water.

A Mudder clutches a trapeze bar after jumping off a twelve-foot-high platform at the King of the Swingers.

Arctic Enema: the clue's in the name.

MUDDER INNOVATOR: Rob Camm

Given my scepticism about how much value my academic study had for my business, I'm enjoying the irony that last year I was invited to help establish and chair the new Centre for Innovation and Entrepreneurship at Bristol University, where I earned my degree. I've relished the opportunity to put what I have learned at Tough Mudder, and some of the best lessons of my time at Harvard, into practice, to put my money where my mouth is. The Bristol initiative is, I think, unique in the academic world. Ours is the first department to offer a syllabus that does not aim to provide a stand-alone business qualification but that instead integrates insights into innovation and entrepreneurship into the university's other courses. Students can take four-year courses in Music with Innovation or Computer Science with Innovation, and so on.

The approach Bristol has taken has allowed us to experiment at the centre in creating a framework of innovation that initiates students in the virtues of the quick and cheap build–measure–learn loop, in terms of their own specializations. It does not aim to teach leadership as a pseudo-science but instead focuses on providing anecdotal insights from people who have established businesses and lived to tell the tale.

As part of my own teaching involvement I launched a competition last year for our undergraduates to design and create a new

Tough Mudder obstacle using our innovation principles. I was privileged to be able to launch this venture on stage alongside Rob Camm, a veteran of two Tough Mudders, who in recent years has learned far more about obstacles and how to innovate to overcome them than anyone in the room. As ever when any two Tough Mudders are gathered together, the thing Rob and I wanted to do most was swap stories. He talked the audience and me through his own history with the event, as a way of introducing the challenge of obstacle creation.

Rob has a special place in Mudder history. In 2015, he became the world's first tetraplegic to complete a Tough Mudder and earn an orange headband. He navigated the course with the help of friends in a pioneering wheelchair that he controls with his chin. Now twenty-two, Rob has been tetraplegic, with no movement in his body from the neck down, since he was a passenger in a car crash in 2013. The crash happened just a week before Rob was due to start as an undergraduate at Bristol, when he was on his way to a party in a friend's car after playing rugby. He subsequently spent ninety-six days in intensive care.

A year later, on a permanent ventilator, and in his specially modified wheelchair, Rob took up his place at the university and is now in his final year studying politics, philosophy and economics. On stage, he explained how his plan was to do postgraduate work to become a lawyer. Before the accident Rob was a committed rugby player, and the thing he missed most, he suggested, was that sense of being part of a team. One of his reasons for doing Tough Mudder was to experience that feeling again. His team included his dad and his sister. 'I was pretty impressed, to be honest, that they both got round, not to mention me,' he says with a smile.

Innovations of all kinds have become a necessity in Rob's

everyday life. He collaborated with physicists and engineers to develop an all-terrain wheelchair like a mini quad bike. The Tough Mudder course was a big test of the vehicle – and also of Rob's stamina. 'It takes quite a lot of endurance,' he suggested, with classic understatement. 'I need so much strength in my neck because I control the chair with my chin, and I have to push that forward all the time. I train by trying to build the strength in my neck by going out in the chair on different paths as much as I can. Just like you would go out for a run to build strength in your legs.'

Mud itself isn't always Rob's enemy. In some ways, a bit of it is good. Hard bumpy ground is tougher, he explains, 'though if the mud gets sticky, then it's a struggle'. Rob has completed two Tough Mudders, and he used the experience of the first to make modifications to his quad-bike chair the second time around. The first time there was a lot of media attention but the second one was more enjoyable, he says, because he could just relax. Obviously, some parts of the course were impossible for him, but he was determined to push himself to try to navigate as much of it as he could. 'In some ways,' he says, 'all my life is like a Tough Mudder. Just getting anywhere requires a lot of planning and a lot of determination. I've always had that determination I think,' he says, 'but obviously it's a bit more necessary now.'

Rob looks to the future with optimism. He places his hope both in the challenges he can overcome and the ingenuity required to get him through them. He is thinking of trying to get up Snowdon, the highest mountain in Wales. 'People tell me it has never been done in a chair like mine, or by someone on a respirator. They just say it is not possible. Which to be honest is probably the worst thing that anyone can say to me.' And he also has faith that scientists will make

advances in the treatment of spinal cord injuries. He recently became the first person in the world with his level of disability to attempt to walk using a pioneering 'skeleton' that is controlled by
brain impulses. Seventy electrodes were attached to his skull and he
was invited to imagine the process of walking: 'left leg up, left leg
forward, left leg down, and so on . . .' The skeleton remains at the
development stage, but Rob retains an innovator's faith in the power
of trial and error: 'If this doesn't work, perhaps the next thing will.'

CHAPTER 6
Founder to CEO: The Challenge of Entrepreneurial Leadership

Whether you think you can, or you think you can't – you're right.

– **Henry Ford**

On my bathroom wall there is a framed letter which reveals that my relationship with Bristol University was not always quite as friendly as it is now. It's a letter I was given by my economics tutor. I say given, because he made a point of calling me out of a lecture and handing it to me in front of all the other students. He appeared to be shaking with anger. The letter reads as follows.

Dear Will:

I am sorry for the late return of these essays. However, my apology is qualified by the fact that your essay on the minimum wage is more than 4,000 words long and your essay on European Monetary Union is more than 3,000 words long. These essays are respectively the longest and second longest essays that I have received this year. It has taken me well over an hour to read and type up my comments on these two essays. Given the importance that I have attached to writing essays that are within the 2,000 word limit, it is totally unacceptable for a student to turn in two essays each of which is more than 1,000 words over this limit.

There is no doubt that you are a student of very considerable ability but you are also one of the most arrogant students I have ever taught. This is reflected not only in the length of your essays but also the style and content. Both of these essays contain numerous fundamental errors and mistakes. These mistakes stem not from any lack of ability or understanding. They result from arrogance which seems, on occasion, to prevent you engaging with either the literature or your lecturer.

In the context of the final exams I doubt this will matter. I fully expect you to graduate with a first. In the context of the labour market the outcome is likely to be very different. No private sector employer will tolerate behaviour of this kind or write you a letter like this, or offer the kind of advice I am trying to give you.

Yours sincerely,
etc.

I guess my tutor – whose ideas I admired and whose lectures I really enjoyed – had a point, though I'd argue with his analysis. I don't think I was arrogant in the way I approached my studies, let alone the 'literature' or the 'lecturer'. It didn't make me at all proud to think I had wasted his time or that I hadn't followed his instruction. He was probably right in saying that future employers might have disapproved of my behaviour. But the fact was I felt I had no choice but to do the essays in the most effective way I knew, otherwise I couldn't see the point of doing the work at all. I wasn't being deliberately rude. I was simply, unconsciously, behaving like an entrepreneur.

I have read many books and been in many lectures where there has been an attempt to describe the qualities that create this semi-mythical character, a reading list that has been emphasized for me of late because I am now tasked with delivering coherent insights on the subject back at Bristol University. In all these studies it often seems to me that the crucial element of that self-selecting character that often gets overlooked is this: entrepreneurs find it almost impossible to do what they are told when the instruction seems arbitrary or perverse. They are not lovers of other people's rules, particularly when those rules get in the way of their own goal. They have great difficulty in 'going through the motions' or 'playing the game'. Or if they do, they will make it abundantly clear that they think the game is a joke.

It's a minor example, but I tend to think of that letter on my bath-room wall when I hear what has become an almost constant demand from political leaders for more 'entrepreneurial ideas'. Or when business leaders or hospital directors or educators argue that 'an en-trepreneurial spirit' needs to be seen in every department of their organization. The people who make those demands should probably be careful what they wish for. Entrepreneurs are rarely able to limit their belief that things can be done better. They are not going to work by their own rules in one area, and be compliant company men in another. In my experience, for better and often for worse, they are not natural employees.

When I was working in counter-terrorism, I often heard people say, 'We need more entrepreneurial thinking in our approach to jihadis.' I completely agreed. As I have written, I was given a lot of responsibility in the Foreign Service at a young age to demonstrate exactly that kind of thinking. That suited me fine. I had some great managers, who were tough on me but showed me a lot of trust and respect and from whom I learned a great deal in terms of strategy and resilience and leadership. For that reason, I am reluctant to criticize the Foreign Office and I am always fiercely defensive if other people do so. But ultimately, the Foreign Office was still part of the British civil service, one of the most hierarchical and bureaucratic institutions ever created (the outlaw drama of James Bond's life starts from that fact). And it eventually became clear I did not fit that structure.

Despite often being singled out for the work I had done when thinking like an entrepreneur, which had produced some tangible successes in the fight against terrorism, I was also informed that the FCO were unable to promote me to a level at which I might have been more effective because I was 'too young'. Ironically, because my project had proved so successful, I had not gone through the conventional career path of a lengthy foreign posting. While in my view that didn't affect my claims, it was made clear that my peers and seniors would not approve. As a compromise the Foreign Service did what they had always done in such situations: they removed me from the role in which I had been effective and sent me to India with a house and servants for a couple of years, effectively marking time until a promotion was age-appropriate. I tried to work in India as I had always done, but my boss there was less inclined to see the value of an entrepreneurial spirit.

When she was away I did my best to take responsibility for setting priorities in her absence. One time, a minor diplomatic crisis came up, and I threw all my efforts into dealing with it. It meant, regrettably, that I was unable to complete some of the work she had asked me to do, including a presentation I had promised to prepare for her. On her return, I explained as clearly as I could what had happened, telling her that I would now complete the work she had assigned me.

She took me to an office and sat me down for an appraisal. She was, much like my old economics tutor, apparently shaking with rage. 'You are,' she informed me, in her precise English accent, 'the laziest, little c – – t I have ever worked with.'

I thought about this judgement for a moment and told her that couldn't be right. She must be mistaken. No one had ever called me 'lazy' or 'little' before. Her three-word appraisal did have an effect though; it made me decide between two courses of action, which I had been weighing up for a while. First, I thought I would act on an ambition to go to Harvard to learn how to run a business. And second, I decided that if I could help it, I would never work for anyone again.

In this sense, I think entrepreneurship is often what is left when you have ruled out all other safer and often more lucrative options for yourself. Much as the culture sometimes tries to insist otherwise, it is, for this reason, not an option for everyone. It is lonely and stressful and pretty much never a shortcut to being rich. For all the abundantly 'creative' possibilities you might feel you have at the outset, the execution of ideas and all the difficulty it involves is all that eventually counts. Making new ideas happen in the real world is generally hard and unglamorous. For this reason, I stress to aspiring entrepreneurs that a start-up should be not so much a choice as a psychological necessity.

At the root of that psychology is a refusal to accept the status quo, a sense that everything – processes, products, services – could be done differently and better or with more energy and fun. Seth Godin, the self-styled marketing maven, calls entrepreneurs heretics. Heretics can't help but see the world as it might be rather than as it is, and they are inspired by the need to persuade others to try to close that gap. I see this heretical habit of mind in many entrepreneurs whom I admire and who have become friends.

It is fundamental, for example, to Neil Blumenthal, who with three friends from Wharton business school founded Warby Parker in 2008. Neil was struck by what you might call a classic heretical 'that just can't be right' moment. His came when he was looking at the things he carried in his pocket, and what struck him was simply this: how can my glasses possibly cost as much as my iPhone? His glasses were made of plastic, they contained no rare earth minerals, and their technology hadn't changed much in a century. And, because they had a tiny designer logo on the side, they cost five hundred dollars. How could that be so?

Blumenthal created a plan that, like all great business plans, became an obsession: to sell beautifully designed glasses for under a hundred dollars. Of course, like my plan for Tough Mudder, that plan did not win the Business Plan Competition at his school. His professors saw mainly problems – the price was too low, people would not buy a personal item like glasses online – but Blumenthal, and his three co-founders, were not put off. He was, he recalls, inspired by the fact that both his grandfathers had been entrepreneurs; they had made him see that 'business was really just problem solving'. And there were always problems to solve (he got around the online problem by sending his customers five pairs of glasses to try for five days, four of which they returned).

Warby Parker has now sold 1.5 million pairs of glasses, and it has done so according to the other founding principles Blumenthal was passionate about: it has a zero carbon footprint and it has distributed a million pairs of glasses to those in need in the developing world through a Buy a Pair, Give a Pair programme. In 2015, the company was valued at $1.2 billion. None of that would have happened had Blumenthal not looked at the objects in his pocket and had a 'that just can't be right' moment.

James Reinhart had a similar thought when he was a student in Boston and looked in his own wardrobe. He wondered idly, and then a bit obsessively, what percentage of his clothing he actually wore and what percentage was just taking up space in his wardrobe. He calculated that about 70 per cent of his clothes were literally a waste of space. And then he did a poll of friends and asked them to check their wardrobes; they came up with a similar percentage. Armed with his 'that just can't be right' fact, Reinhart resolved to change the way we buy, wear and store clothing.

His idea for thredUP, which offered an easy way to clear out wardrobes and to repair, sell and distribute quality clothes, was rejected by thirty banks and venture capitalists. Reinhart wasn't discouraged, because he was a heretic: he knew there was a problem that needed fixing in how we all lived, and he believed he had a solution to it. Eventually, he found some funding and got thredUP off the ground. In 2015, Goldman Sachs invested $81 million in his business, which now operates across the United States. Reinhart suggests that thinking like an entrepreneur is thinking about 'how the world looks today, and about what can make it ten times better'.

We didn't hear much of those kinds of simple messages at Harvard Business School. But it was the kind of conversation that I would have after class with Jennifer Hyman, one of the only other entrepreneurs I met at Harvard. Jenn and I bonded over our shared interest in deflating the egos of some of our more entitled 'master of the universe' classmates and through our obsessive enthusiasm for our heretical start-up ideas.

Jenn had come up with her idea for Rent the Runway at almost the same time as I had first thought about Tough Mudder, so we spent a lot of time scouring the curriculum for ideas that might be helpful and refining our business plans. Her heretical mission was to democratize high fashion by creating a service that rented haute couture fashion to women. Jenn is an honorary Tough Mudder in that she showed resilience and faith in her idea in the face of scepticism and obstacles. I think she and I were the only two graduates in our year to launch our own businesses upon graduating.

Rent the Runway began in 2009 with twenty-eight designer brands and no warehouse. They stored their dresses at a dry cleaner's four blocks from the office. As with Tough Mudder, Jenn hit the ground running. An article in *The New York Times* led to a hundred thousand members signing up in her first week of business, and she had a million members just over a year after launch. Today Jenn employs 850 people and has a 160,000 square-foot warehouse in New Jersey that houses the largest dry cleaner's in the United States; she works with 340 of the world's top designers. A recent article in

Cosmopolitan suggested, without irony, that she had, in a few short years, achieved the not inconsiderable task of 'changing the way women shop for ever'. Throughout that journey since Harvard, Jenn and I have met up and swapped experiences and challenged each other regarding what we could be doing differently or better.

One of the things all these entrepreneurs share, I think, is a sense that, looking back, they hardly had a choice in what they did. The business they wanted to create effectively chose them. They just enthusiastically embraced their fate.

That's also true of me and Tough Mudder. The motivation to be an entrepreneur is often boiled down to the cliché that you must above all follow your passion. I don't think that phrase quite gets what I am describing. If I hear people say things like 'I want to set up a ski company because skiing is my passion,' I can't help feeling they are likely to be disappointed. If they run a ski company, they are going to spend an awful lot of time in an office, talking about skis. They would probably be better off, if they really wanted to follow their passion, to get a job where they have lots of spare time and can live near a mountain.

When Jenn Hyman or Neil Blumenthal or James Reinhart describe their respective passions, it is not often about the product or even the environment they have created (though they are proud of those things). It is about the way their business has proved that their original idea about making the world a slightly more enjoyable and efficient place was right all along. The products themselves were just a vehicle for delivering that idea.

When I think of my own early efforts at commercial enterprises, I could certainly convince myself there was a pattern in what I was trying to prove. That I was being led to the problems I think

I eventually tried to address with Tough Mudder. I set up three businesses at school and university. The first was when I was fourteen and part of what was called a 'Young Enterprise scheme', an initiative to encourage entrepreneurial thinking in schools. Most people made biscuits or cushions and sold them at school events, making about a hundred pounds. The team I led managed to get the concession for a nail polish that changed colour under UV light from a company in the States by creating a web page – this was 1997 – that suggested we were older than we were. The earliest leadership decision of my business career was to manoeuvre the teacher who was supervising us out of the decision-making process. And we sold about four thousand pounds' worth of this nail polish around town (with the aid of a UV lamp borrowed from the science labs). For a few months among the teenagers of Kettering, it was the must-have accessory. Everyone wanted to be a member of that nail-polish tribe.

The second business came about after I persuaded my headmaster to let me send out a letter to all the parents at school, suggesting that their sons and daughters needed a sports bag branded with the Oundle school emblem and name. The letter, which I still have, wasn't perfectly written, but it was well worded enough to suggest that while the bags were not mandatory, kids might feel a bit left out if they did not have one. I mentioned as a further incentive that students at a rival school had branded bags. After a bit of legwork and bargaining I found a supplier in Hull, in the north of England, who could supply these bags for three pounds, and I sold them to parents at a still reasonable twenty pounds. When I came back to school early for pre-season rugby training, I went to the headmaster's office and asked, 'Did anyone order the bags?' He came out with a huge box stuffed full of letters, and I remember sitting on my bed going through all the orders. Basically, every boy in the school had bought one. I made ten thousand pounds.

At university in Bristol – when I wasn't writing overlong essays for my economics class – I started a similar business. I had an idea for a T-shirt that had course subjects printed on the back and the names of all the people studying that subject listed underneath in small type. These T-shirts are quite common now, but at the time, no one had seen them before and they sold extremely well. I expanded to other campuses and colleges around the country. People could never work out how I got all the names of the people taking that course, but it was pretty simple. I'd take a high-res picture of the bulletin board outside a lecture hall, which routinely listed the names of students studying a particular subject. I'd then e-mail the photos to an outsourcing company and someone in the Philippines printed up the shirts for me.

These little businesses were just hobbies, though I took them seriously – and at one point thought about making the T-shirt enterprise a full-time occupation. Somewhere underneath I think I wanted to prove that despite all the academic complexities of my economics course – which I loved – a business boiled down to a few basic equations: you think about what people might want to buy, you make a product, you figure out how much it costs to make it, you figure out how much you can sell it for, and then you sell it. Then you look at how much time you spent on all that and you decide whether that was a good use of your time.

Beyond that equation, with the bags and the T-shirts in particular, I was increasingly interested in the way you could sell the idea of communality, how you could create a business out of shared identities – even just the must-have factor of nail varnish or a bag or a T-shirt – and how you could quickly make that tribal, viral idea spread. They were all little test cases for a more grown-up business based on that universal need: belonging.

Many definitions of social enterprises would not include for-profit organizations like Tough Mudder, which sell ideas of community along with their product. I believe that is a false opposition. Businesses can deliver values and happiness and well-being just as surely as charities or government agencies. Entrepreneurs should apply their problem-solving talents to social questions as well as markets. Clearly Tough Mudder is not in the business of curing cancer or bringing peace to the Middle East. But I believe that it has found one way of aligning its commercial success with some real human and societal needs. On one level we are in the events business, selling weekend obstacle courses. On another we are part of a trend that makes health and vivid experiences the new luxury goods. But I think at the core what we are offering are those hard-to-find and much-in-demand qualities: community and self-belief.

At Harvard, I played around with a few of these thoughts. Quite early on, and by accident, I introduced a new sport to the university. The sport was a version of the ancient Indian game of *kabaddi*, which involves capturing territory and raiding parties and, curiously, not taking a breath while in the opposition's part of the field. It was said to have been the sport of Lord Krishna himself. I'd learned to play kabaddi while I was stationed in India with the Foreign Office. I mentioned the game at one point in a seminar at Harvard and was met by the alpha males in my section with a bit of predictable mocking and derision. 'What's Will railing about now?' To me that response sounded something like a challenge, so I invited my classmates outside for a kabaddi lesson. I'm not sure how well this story reflects on me, but when I mentioned this chapter about heretical – Tough Mudder – leadership to Jenn Hyman she insisted I include it. I'll tell it, in that case, mostly as she remembers it.

Jenn recalls how I led the section out on the field and divided it into teams and had them chanting 'KABADDI! KABADDI!' in low and high voices. She explains how I instructed them in the game's unfamiliar, aggressive poses and karate kicks, performed with shirts off, facing each other. At this point her memory captures more details than mine. 'Basically, you took a bunch of thirty-year-old men and quickly made them act like five-year-olds,' she claims. 'They seemed to love it. That wasn't the end of it though. You told them, "We are going to do this once a week and we are going to attract more people." This built up to a crescendo – and I have photos – when all of the men in our entire year were gathered outside the prestigious Baker Library to play a kabaddi tournament. Chanting. Squaring up to each other. Doing the weird martial arts. All the women had been invited and were just laughing and wondering what the heck was going on. I thought it was one of the most hilarious things I had ever seen. These guys were all taking it immensely seriously. You were roaming the field, urging them on: "Kabaddi! Kabaddi!"'

Jenn recalls, too, another moment that I don't remember. She watched me, she claims, looking out over a field containing at least four hundred shirtless men acting like idiots, many of whom thought they were (measured in zeros) the smartest males in the world. She swears she whispered to me, 'Will, what is this?' Apparently, I looked back at her with a raised eyebrow and said, 'Jenn, it's alpha males.' Jenn is in touch with more of those kabaddi players than I am. By all accounts they remember the kabaddi season fondly to this day.

Jenn further insists that Tough Mudder could never have come about if it hadn't been for my version of kabaddi at Harvard. I'm not at all sure about that, but I would go as far as to say it was another, jokey test of my interest in the seductive power of tribes. Mostly I was having a bit of fun with the high seriousness of many of those guys, their sense that everything was a competition and an opportunity to display their manly prowess. But it also revealed something else: something that made me think. I'd managed to create this weekly event with just a silly challenge and a partly made up set of rituals and rules. What if you used those principles more in earnest, challenged people to believe in something as passionately as you believed in it; what might be possible then?

Heretics tend, Seth Godin claims, to use the language of faith: 'Challenging the status quo requires a commitment, both public and private,' he writes. 'It involves reaching out to others and putting your ideas on the line. Heretics must believe. More than anyone else in an organization, it's the person who's challenging the status quo who must have confidence in her beliefs.'

That sense of unshakeable belief in the viability of your idea is crucial because it feeds the resilience that gets any new project or business off the ground and encourages the grit that sees it start to thrive. The idea of making money is not in itself sustaining. There has to be the stronger motivation that you are doing something worthwhile and interesting with your life and spreading those qualities to the lives of others. Without that core belief you would never keep going.

Neil Blumenthal at Warby Parker did not believe in a new kind of eyeglasses; he believed he could make a difference in the world with a new kind of business model. Jenn Hyman does not see Rent the

Runway as a shop or a service but as a 'life mission', which is 'to make women feel beautiful and self-confident every day and by nature of doing that to be empowered to change their lives, to ask for the promotion and get the guy and achieve what they want to achieve'.

Missions are essential to entrepreneurs. I was affected as I was setting out on the journey to Tough Mudder by reading former presidential candidate Ross Perot's extraordinary account of his extraordinary life. Perot's singular obsession with problem solving had seen him become both the 'fastest, richest Texan' and the biggest loser in the history of the New York Stock Exchange on a single day. Later in life he invested both in Steve Jobs and in hostage release – to prove his point that there were always solutions – and never stopped trying to remake the world a little more efficiently. 'Failures,' he wrote, 'are like skinned knees – painful but superficial.' Even so, the things he remembered of his career, and the things you remember from his account of it, were not the successes but the number of times people said no to him – seventy-seven – before he got his first sale and how often he literally risked everything to prove his belief in his business ideas – to the extent that his wife threatened to divorce him and his family disowned him.

Perot was an extreme case. But I recognized from his story the sense that any entrepreneurial mission is non-negotiable. The best test of any idea is the realization that you will never be happy in your life until you have at least given it your best shot. The moment you are struck with that realization is the moment when you understand you are perhaps wired slightly differently from most people. Confirmation of that comes when you have to explain for the fiftieth time why you are not doing the easy thing, like using your talent and experience to get a salaried job, but instead are obsessed with this strange thing that is not even a thing except in your head: mud runs, in 2009, in America, in my case.

All entrepreneurs probably know that feeling – and the slightly pitying look on the face of people who don't quite get it. At the very start of Tough Mudder, when I was mostly working on my own, I would go for drinks with friends from Harvard. They would listen to me talk about my heretical and muddy mission with a slightly disbelieving look – 'What's Will talking about now?' – and when it came to paying the bill they would say, 'I'll get this,' as if I had become a no-hope charity case. 'It's not that bad!' I would insist. 'I can afford to buy a round.'

That sense of disbelief, the idea that I might come to my senses and go to work for a consultancy, persisted long after Tough Mudder launched. When I met up with friends, they would tell me about their frustrations with their boss or a tough presentation they had to give or whatever, and I would explain how I was in a stand-off with New Jersey contractors who were holding our equipment hostage in their van until we paid them. Or how I had discovered that the people who had offered us a deal on renting portable toilets were actually mobsters who had no portable toilets but wanted payment anyway.

One of the things that often came up when we were discussing business ethics at Harvard was the 'Nigeria question'. That is the one that asks, 'What would happen to your company values of decency and transparency if, say, you were in Lagos and you needed to get a bridge built quickly?' The answer is always, 'Well, things are a bit different in Nigeria.' But in my daily experience things were a bit different if you went four miles through the Holland Tunnel. The high-level problems that you think you are solving with your business are not the problems that overwhelm you day by day.

It is not the major setbacks that get to you; it is the accumulation of small ones. I didn't cry often when we set up Tough Mudder (after all, as the pledge says, 'I do not whine – kids whine') but one time was just before the second event when we had been hit by Mr Mouse's writ and were coming to terms with the full logistical nightmare of what we had committed to.

I was at a post office in New York, and it was imperative that we mail some large parcels of equipment for the California team that night. We got to the post office with the parcels with ten minutes to spare but were informed that when you send a package, it can't have any writing on it other than the address. So we had to buy brown paper to rewrap and readdress the packages, and by the time we had done that the woman pulled down the shutter and said we were too late. It was after five p.m., and we had missed the next-day delivery. We were tired. There had been, it seemed, a thousand things conspiring against us that week. And I felt tears welling up. It wasn't the worst thing that happened. But it was the last thing that happened.

During despairing moments, and all entrepreneurs have plenty of them, it is your sense of mission that keeps you going. In the difficult transition from founding a company to the day-to-day dramas of leading it, it is essential to keep that founding principle in mind. To a large degree that means falling back on your core values. I tried to always be clear and consistently principled when it came to some of the tougher situations regarding contracts and negotiation. I tried to behave at all times like a Tough Mudder.

A couple of days before our first event of the second year, for example, our contractor put down his tools and refused to carry on until we paid him for materials he said he had paid for already.

The contract we had signed stated we would pay him twenty thousand dollars up front, as we had done, and the balance twenty-eight days after completion. He wanted the balance – eighty thousand dollars, I think – then and there, or, he said, the course would not get built. If he had come to me and asked to renegotiate or said he had a specific cash problem, I would have listened and maybe would have compromised. As the contractor knew, however, we had ten thousand people arriving in two days' time to run a course that had not been built. He gambled on me doing the easy thing and paying up. But I don't like to be threatened. It sets bad precedents. To his surprise, I told him on the spot that his demands were out of line and his services were no longer needed. After a slightly panicky search, we managed to find another contractor, the Policelli family, who could build the course at short notice and who have become a crucial and trusted part of our story.

In those kinds of negotiations, you use what you can. I think there was an advantage to me and Guy Livingstone being British. We could use cultural differences to our advantage or as an excuse. The naivety and innocence that come with being an outsider can be useful allies. Guy maintained that had we stayed in England, we would never have started the business, because we would have been more aware of the negative voices in our heads: 'England has been much more of a trading economy where establishing careers in finance, law and accounting are the keys to success,' he once suggested. 'This is different from America, where it is the big dream to build something from nothing. It seems as if entrepreneurship is more deeply ingrained in the culture than it is where Will and I were raised.' There's some truth in that.

As well as those advantages, there were unforeseen conse-quences in trying to set up a business – and lead a tribe – in a foreign country. A good deal of that came down to the old saying that Brit-ain and the United States are two nations divided by a common language.

My favourite example came one afternoon when I was standing talking to a couple of venue owners in Upstate New York about events we were thinking of creating and whether they would be interested in being involved. I was talking about doing a Tough Mudder Half and described it in relation to the popularity of duathlons – a duath-lon being a triathlon without the swim. I could see the venue owners looking increasingly alarmed as I explained this concept, and I couldn't quite think why. Eventually one of them couldn't contain his disbelief. 'You talk about "duathlons",' he said, using my British pro-nunciation, 'but are you sure a triathlon aimed exclusively at Jewish people would even be a possibility in this country?'

Language difficulties aside, there were plenty of challenges in translating my vision for the company to the reality of leading it. The entrepreneurial mind-set, which drives innovative change, is not al-ways best suited to the inevitable compromises and difficulties of leading a team. I think I expect a lot of myself, and I am aware that I can feel let down by people who don't share that sense of mission. My wife, Katie, recently said something to me which resonated. We were talking about the rights and wrongs of whether I should go out of my way to compromise in a certain situation. Katie suggested, with a laugh, that I was actually quite a straightforwardly ethical person: 'If someone's been an arsehole in your eyes, it's perfectly ac-ceptable for you to be an arsehole back to them.' She knows me too well. I do my best to avoid conflict, but if I find myself confronted I don't, for better and worse, find it easy to back down.

One solution to this for me as a leader was to try to make our organization a haven for those who shared that attitude to the world: people who could take responsibility and initiative, who were frustrated by bureaucracy and hierarchy but who had a very clear understanding of our deeper purpose and values. There are consequences to this style of leadership, and they are exacerbated when the founder continues in the company as CEO, as I have done. Concentrating on values rather than processes, and trying to instil those values in a very hands-on way – through Tough Mudder University, for example – rather than outsourcing that responsibility to others means that you are often seen as the personification of all that the company stands for. That can feel like quite an exposed position. If an employee is feeling unfulfilled in their work for whatever reason, or under-appreciated in some way, they tend not to blame the company or the system; they blame you.

We did an anonymous employee engagement survey a couple of years ago. The results were unambiguous. It wasn't that half the people in the company were somewhat happy and half were a bit grumpy. Ninety per cent of people were extremely happy and 10 per cent were extremely unhappy, and there was nothing in between. Afterwards I talked to all the staff about those results. I told them that we made the survey anonymous so there would be no consequence to any negative reports. But also, that if you were among the 10 per cent who really didn't like it here, I had to say that, honestly, that fact was unlikely to change. Still, on the bright side, there was an obvious solution. The same solution I followed when I decided to leave the Foreign Office after my unambiguous appraisal.

Some of the people who were unhappy were completely out-raged by this idea. They came to see me one by one. 'Will, you're telling me that if I'm unhappy I've got to leave?'

'No,' I said, 'I'm not saying that at all. But you should never forget it is an option. Empowerment works both ways. We try to create an organization at Tough Mudder where people can take responsibility and thrive, where they are encouraged to learn from mistakes and not be blamed for them. Where they feel that they have a real stake in any successes. But we, like any organization, do not have the power to make every individual who works here content and ful-filled. That part – finding out how to be happy – is not our responsi-bility. It has to come from you.'

I think a couple of years before I wouldn't necessarily have had the conviction to deliver that particular message to an employee. When I first tried to lead Tough Mudder, if someone came to me and said that they were unhappy my first thought would have been, *Well what can we do to make you more content?* How can we change our ways? One of the things you learn about leadership the longer you practise it is the fact that though you can try to nurture a culture in which people feel that they have a stake and in which you hope they can thrive, not everyone will seize that chance. I don't think the solution to that is to try to modify the way you work so everyone feels at home with it. I think it is your role to be consistent to the values that culture emphasizes and try to communicate the reasons behind them. Values can't be tailored to fit everyone. If somebody doesn't want to take responsibility for the work they have been given or wants to be hand-held through it or needs to be constantly singled out for special praise, then there are probably other organizations that will suit them better. In this sense, the Tough Mudder events themselves offer another metaphor for the company; though every-one is completely welcome at them, they are very clearly not for everybody. Some take one look at our obstacles and can't wait to get stuck in. Plenty of other people run a mile in the other direction.

I started this chapter by suggesting that entrepreneurs find it hard to live by other people's rules. That is not the same as living by no rules at all, however. James Kerr writes in his book about the All Blacks: 'Wise leaders seek to understand how the brain reacts to stress and practise simple, almost meditative techniques to stay calm, clear and connected. They use maps, mantras and anchors to navigate their way through highly pressurized situations, both personal and professional, and to bring themselves back to the mo-ment. In this way they and their teams stay on top of their game and on top of the situation.'

I used to try to lead as much as possible through instinct. With a small team made up mostly of people I had come of age with in the business, it was possible. But as the complexity of the business and the number of staff grew, it quickly became clear that instinct alone wouldn't be enough. I have found the advice contained in James Kerr's observation useful as I've tried to grow Tough Mudder from its original 'business of belonging' roots. For most of that time I carried the mission and principles of leadership style in my head, but to find some consistency a while back I decided it might be a useful exercise to clear a day or two to think exactly what those principles should be. The *kaizen* credo had defined the culture of the office, and the Mudder pledge was a statement of intent for our tribe, but what were the rules of engagement that I might best use to lead the business and keep it on track? In the end, I wrote down five rules and pared them down as much as possible:

- Be Bold: Push through big ideas and patiently build consensus. Don't fear failure or avoid difficult conversations.
- Stay Focused: Don't procrastinate. Focus energy solely on achieving goals and priorities. Be willing to say no and cut losses when necessary.
- Live in the Now: Don't put too much pressure on yourself to do everything all at once. Make time for others – particularly family.
- Act Rationally: Don't take things personally. Keep problems in perspective. Evaluate your own emotions when making decisions.
- Be Positive: Focus on others' strengths (not weaknesses). Avoid being judgemental. Focus on the future, not the past. Be grateful for all you have.

I keep these thoughts on my to-do list and try to review them at least once a week. Quite often, I have the feeling that they keep me sane.

MUDDER LEADERS:
Seven-Day Warriors

It's been important, given that Tough Mudder was partially inspired by the military-style psychological training I had gone through in the Foreign Office, and our links with Special Forces' challenges, that we should have a strong bond with veterans and veterans' charities. Much of our Mudder spirit – No Mudder Left Behind – is based on that ethos of collective responsibility. Veterans identified with Tough Mudder too. From the beginning, we had interest in the event from lots of enlisted and former soldiers, who used Tough Mudder to get their fitness levels up or to rehabilitate – or just because. My understanding of leadership has evolved from the best of those examples, of never asking someone to do anything you would not be prepared to do yourself, of trying to lead through the example of clear-thinking strategy and courage, remembering that you are only ever as good as the weakest link in your team.

We formalized our emotional relationship with these values by partnering with the major charities that supported soldiers injured by the wars in the Middle East and Afghanistan. The strength of those partnerships is bolstered by wounded veterans being very visible in nearly all of our events; and their attitudes prove infectious. This association was encouraged by the example of a few extraordinary individuals. One was Noah Galloway, who had been severely injured in an IED attack in Iraq in 2005. Noah lost his left arm below the elbow and his left leg below the knee. He went on to be a multiple Tough Mudder and also won third place on *Dancing with the Stars* and led his team to victory on the American TV series *Grit*. We made Noah our first official 'Muddervator' in 2015. It was awe-inspiring to see him not only hauling himself around the course, with his prosthetic leg and one arm – even swinging through the Funky Monkey bars – but also helping others at every turn.

Before he ran his first Mudder in 2011, Noah had been reading obsessively about the event. 'I started reading article after article about Tough Mudder and I read a lot about injured veterans who came out to these events,' he recalls. 'But what I read was these vets weren't finishing. They were out there to raise money and awareness for various organizations, but they weren't running and completing the course. I thought *How hard can it be?* This motivated me. I had something to prove.'

Noah did complete the course that year, despite his prosthesis coming loose and having to be held together with a makeshift emergency repair for the last three miles. He has done many more Mudders since.

Noah's pioneering efforts inspired many other wounded veterans to train to complete Tough Mudders. Mark Holloway, another of our ambassadors, based in the United Kingdom, admits he felt a little humbled when he saw Galloway's feats. 'I've been reading Noah's book,' he says. 'I look at him and he has lost one arm and one leg. He's still phenomenally fit and he does it all. I just look at that and think: I have got no excuse.'

It was seeing people who were worse off than he was in the Royal Centre for Defence Medicine in Birmingham, England, that helped Mark shrug off his own severe injuries, sustained while on his third tour of duty in Afghanistan in 2010. He had been leading his platoon of the Rifles regiment on patrol when he was blown up by an IED. The bomb went off right next to him, and the blast ripped through his forearm, severing a radial artery and causing catastrophic bleeding. Despite this, Mark organized his own recovery by radioing through instructions to a US Special Forces helicopter to pick him up. 'By that point,' he says, 'as platoon sergeant I was so used to doing a casualty evacuation for my guys that were injured that when it came to me being the injured person I just did my own. I'd seen more blood in my three tours than Rambo. I went through all the protocols while I was pouring blood into the ground. It was just natural.' Mark almost died from the bleeding, and once he got back to the hospital it was unclear if his arm could be saved.

After a series of operations and a long period of rehabilitation, he did manage to regain use of his arm, though he has lost two of the muscles in his forearm, and he has no sensation in his upper arm. He made the decision to start raising money for Help for Heroes in part because he felt he had got off so lightly: 'I kind of felt a little bit guilty because the treatment and attention that I was receiving when I was in the same hospital and same rehabilitation department was the same as for guys who had no legs,' he says. 'So that was the turning point for me.'

When he subsequently took up a job as colour sergeant at the Royal Military Academy Sandhurst, Tough Mudder became his vehicle for raising money and awareness. 'I spent a year in recovery and then at the end of that before I went back to work I did a Tough Mudder with my brother – the first event in the UK in 2012 – to raise money for Help for Heroes. From there on the hunger grew to want to do more and to compete in World's Toughest and to push myself more each year.'

One of the things he appreciates about running the events is the opportunity they give for soldiers to run alongside civilian participants. Since the wars began there haven't been that many chances for the general population to show their appreciation for the sacrifices some of the military have made, so Mark and his teams receive a lot of encouragement. The same goes for Wounded Warriors and Team Rubicon in the States, who get a special shout-out at the Tough Mudder starting line.

'It's definitely a good support,' Mark says. 'You hear people cheering you on when they see your running T-shirt, Help for Heroes. I think it touches a nerve with people especially when we were so heavily involved in Afghanistan.'

The other response he gets is people suggesting that he must find the courses a breeze after all his military training. He suggests that is far from the case.

'They say, yeah, you are used to doing this stuff with a helmet on and a weapon and gear. But it's a completely different thing. People tell me any soldier should be able to run World's Toughest, and I am like, no, not really. Not at all. It's a twenty-four-hour event and it takes a year to train for it if you want to do well.' In his first year, Mark didn't train for it. He decided to go to World's Toughest with two weeks' notice. The aim was just to survive. 'I had a box of doughnuts and a flask of coffee and just went for it,' he recalls. He's learned a lot since then, and now he sees the event like a big family reunion. Last year Mark had the British 'super volunteers' Guy and Miranda Richardson as his pit crew, and their presence has become a regular fixture: 'They live and breathe it. They are amazing people. They are flying out with me this time to support me again.'

Mark was posted to Edinburgh last year, so he is away from his family and young son during the week. 'I have those hills literally less than a mile away from my accommodation. So I am up there most days; it's perfect Tough Mudder country. Yesterday afternoon, for example, I was there for six hours in the afternoon just running around the hills and the lakes.'

When he gets home on the weekends, his little boy greets him with the words 'Daddy's been running.'

'I never admit to being good,' Mark says, with typical Mudder understatement. 'I'm just persistent. But still, the level that I am at now, I've never got to that in anything else in my life and it's a good feeling that I can actually do that now.'

In that sense, he says, doing Tough Mudder has given him a focus and a purpose that he has rarely experienced before. He doesn't look back at all, except to count his blessings.

'I went in the army at sixteen,' he says. 'I wasn't that interested in school. I was a fit young lad and for me the natural thing to do was to join up. I wouldn't change anything about it, even getting blown up, because I believe the person that I am now is partly down to nearly dying in Afghanistan, and the injuries I sustained have shaped my future and the person that I am. Part of that is being a Tough Mudder. Anything different and it wouldn't be me.'

CHAPTER 7
The Business of Belonging: Connecting the Tribe

I get by with a little help from my friends.

– **Ringo Starr**

If you remove a single cell from a human heart you can watch that cell carry on beating on its own under a microscope for several days. If you add a cell from another human heart to the first, the two communicate in interesting ways. Though the two cells are beating at different rates when they are put together, they quickly start to beat in time when they get close to touching. And when they touch they tend to keep on beating longer than they would apart. Add more cells from different hearts and the same thing happens. Quite soon all the heart cells are beating with each other strongly in time. Some scientists have speculated that this subconscious adaptive rhythm may begin to explain how social animals bond from birth – and perhaps even how tribes begin to form.

Tribes differ from other groups, in the way we think of them at Tough Mudder, because they exhibit a stronger human bond than simple social networks. Individual tribe members are encouraged to express their full potential, but in the context of the values shared by the wider group. There are always two competing positive forces in any functioning society. One force is cooperation: people are healthier and happier – and perhaps wealthier – when they collaborate. The other is competition: personal striving to be the best creates the most successful communities by spreading aspiration and prosperity. In my view these forces work best when they are held in tension. If cooperation is the only driver, there is not enough of the spark and energy of the individual. If selfishness dominates, you lose the social power of altruistic networks and connected tribes.

The Olympic Games are an interesting case study. The games are, of course, a celebration of extreme personal achievement, measured in fractions of millimetres and hundredths of seconds. But in all of this triumph and defeat there are memorable expressions of a communal spirit too.

In Rio 2016, the most celebrated example of this spirit came in the semi-final of the women's 5,000 metres. With one lap to go, New Zealand's Nikki Hamblin and Abbey D'Agostino of the United States tripped over each other and fell heavily onto the track. Their genuine hopes of making the final – to which they had dedicated years of effort and sacrifice – went down with them. They would have been forgiven for cursing their luck or cursing each other. Instead, Hamblin, first to her feet, did not try to catch up with the race; she stopped to check on her injured rival. She then helped D'Agostino up – the American had torn her cruciate ligament – and supported her to the finishing line.

That moment affected everyone who saw it. It was shared on social media just as often as Usain Bolt's victory grin or Mo Farah's eye-bulging sprint finish. It affected us in part because it was a moment of true sportsmanship in all the 'race-face' focus of an Olympic semi-final. But more important was that it was done spontaneously. Hamblin and D'Agostino didn't think twice about where their priorities lay. They weren't denying the thrill of pushing themselves as hard as they could – they had devoted their lives to that – but they also were courageous enough to know that sometimes other values, and other people, were just as important. Sport matters because, ultimately, it doesn't matter.

I've mentioned how one of the light-bulb moments for the creation of Tough Mudder was the experience during a triathlon when I couldn't free a stuck zip on my wetsuit, and – comically – no one was prepared to give up the couple of seconds it would have required to help me. Set against this was another experience. When I lived in London and was working for the FCO, I used to go kite surfing as often as I could at a place called Hayling Island on the south coast. The sport was quite new in the United Kingdom, and I loved the physicality and adrenaline rush of it. All that was made possible, though, by the camaraderie of the early adopters.

Kite-surfing equipment has evolved a lot since then, but in those days it was almost impossible to launch a kite on your own. You had to ask someone to hold your kite into the wind while you clipped yourself into the harness to get started. This was a relatively small thing to ask, but you felt like you were being a real pal to someone by doing it – and they were being a real pal to you for doing the same. Out of these small acts of generosity and kindness a very strong community was quickly created. Beginner or veteran, the kite surfers of Hayling Island were all looking for some personal thrills but were also all in it together.

When I started Tough Mudder I found a lot of other people who had come to this idea by different routes, both among early partici-pants and in the team in the office. Tough Mudder attracted surfers and climbers in disproportionate numbers because they understood the value of mutual cooperation to achieve a tough physical chal-lenge. Alex Patterson, our original in-house lawyer – and do-or-die obstacle-tester – loved it because it reminded him of his years as a lifeguard on a beach on Long Island.

'Lifeguarding is in a lot of ways like Tough Mudder,' Alex sug-gests now. 'It's athletic but it's not a competition. You work hard and play hard, and no one's above having a beer or two after getting off the stand at night. But most important no lifeguard swims out to a victim and says, "I'm going to race you back in." In Tough Mudder, it's a bit the same. Stronger Mudders might sit up there on one of the walls and spend twenty minutes helping people over, and you have this same feeling of satisfaction and connection, of literally offering a hand.'

There are, of course, wider lessons in this fact. It probably explains why the event has resonated among groups that prize high-performance teamwork: military servicemen and -women, firefighters, police offi-cers, teachers and nurses, people who know all about the satisfaction of relying on each other to help others. But it also explains the appeal to people whose day jobs don't offer that camaraderie but who crave some of it in their lives.

My early research suggested that one response to the financial crash of 2008, and the austerity politics that followed, was a sharply increased focus on health and fitness. Having lost some control in one important aspect of their lives – jobs and money – people tried to exert a bit more control over another aspect: their bodies.

This trend had been strengthening for a while, of course, with the growth of marathons and 10Ks and Pilates and spin classes and all the rest. But at the same time, it seemed to me that not all that exercise was doing what it was designed to do. Rather than being an escape from the pressures and stresses of work, at its extreme it looked like another expression of them.

Don't get me wrong – I'm all for being in good shape and living healthily. I exercise pretty much every day, try to eat a balanced diet, and I couldn't be without the sense of well-being that lifestyle provides. I love the idea of pushing yourself to find your limits and then going beyond them. But it sometimes felt like many of the workaholics I knew (and I was sometimes guilty of this myself) were in danger of taking all their obsessive habits to the treadmill. Joe De Sena at Spartan Race sometimes talks about a few per cent of excess body fat in terms of good and evil. That seemed to me a little extreme. Some gym regimes seemed to encourage a 'subway mentality'. Everyone was plugged into a headset or watching TV while they trained staring into a mirror. They sweated next to other people sweating without once making eye contact. And where was the fun in that?

We wanted Tough Mudder to offer another way of doing things, for a few reasons. An overriding one was a belief that total self-reliance, while a great thing in many ways, will never make us happy on its own. Sometimes we have to risk pitching in with everybody else, just for the hell of it, and see where we end up. Contemporary life, with its gated living and insistence on virtual rather than actual communities, often seemed to resist that idea. Adam Grant, the author of *Give and Take*, whose ideas have been an inspiration to our business, suggests that 'Americans see independence as a symbol of strength, viewing interdependence as a sign of weakness.' At Tough Mudder we wondered if that balance might just shift a little.

I'd developed an understanding of the benefits of greater balance between those forces, as I've tried to set out in this book, from various experiences growing up, and in the Foreign Office and at Harvard. There was plenty of research to back up this understanding. Grant, a professor at the Wharton School, broadly divides people into three groups by their dominant behaviour: There are 'Takers' (we all know a few) who make it their life's work to receive more from others than they give in return. Then, second, there are people who display 'matching behaviour' who live by a principle of fairness and who believe that one good turn deserves another ('Matchers' understand that cooperation makes the world go around: you help me and I'll help you). And then there are the 'Givers'. These are people who routinely go out of their way to do more than is demanded of them, even when there is no prospect of personal gain. They don't do cost–benefit analysis of their actions. They give because they believe in, and thrive on, giving.

Grant has done long-term studies of how these philosophies play out in the real – commercial – world. The conclusions are fascinating. Not surprisingly, perhaps, most people display a version of matching behaviour that puts them in the centre of the graph of success, measured in terms of financial reward. Takers, meanwhile, often do well in the short term, but over a longer period their philosophy is less successful as Matchers work out that they are being ripped off.

The outlier group in this study, though, are the Givers. No one will be surprised that Givers tend to occupy the lowest percentiles of the success graph – after all, they give more effort, more time, more commitment than the others without expectation of anything in return – and that is often how it turns out.

But there is a counter-intuitive fact. Those who end up consistently at the very top of the graph, who achieve the greatest rewards, are Givers too. They are people for whom nothing is too much trouble. As the great American philosopher Ralph Waldo Emerson wrote, 'It is one of the most beautiful compensations of this life that no man can sincerely try to help another without helping himself.' Grant shows these benefits are likely to be material as well as leading to greater contentment.

We all know a few Givers in our lives, people who willingly do so much that they make us feel a bit hopeless for what we offer. One of my own examples is Sarah Robb O'Hagan, who until recently was president of the Equinox fitness group, whose brands include Pure Yoga and SoulCycle. Sarah is one of those people who, when you ask her for a bit of help with something in a one-line e-mail, will send seven thoughtful and encouraging paragraphs of advice within minutes and then subsequently hooks you up with all sorts of ideas and people who might help with your problem. She doesn't sometimes go the extra mile; she always does. We invited Sarah, a multiple Tough Mudder, to talk about her philosophy at our last annual company weekend retreat in Upstate New York. She stole the show.

Sarah left Equinox last year to set up Extreme You. The project aims to inspire and mentor millennials and twentysomethings who are looking for more meaning and direction in their lives. Sarah's research suggests that this group is less inclined than earlier generations to put itself on the line or make itself vulnerable. 'It's tough for this generation who have been helicopter-parented through school and then on graduating are told "go and find your passion",' she says. 'In my experience, people who are very passionate in their work originally just got stuck in at something to start with and worked for hours and hours at it. The effort itself generated the passion. And they found that worked in all areas of their lives. They give things a go. That's the reason it makes me really happy that something like Tough Mudder is doing well in the world. It finds the people who have it in them to challenge themselves, and gives them the role models and opportunity to go for it.'

Sarah's passion for Extreme You is infectious. I think the project reveals a lot about the relationship between personal ambition and the barriers to success. Some of this has had to do with the evolution in how we communicate. The generation that has grown up with digital media has become used to relatively one-sided risk-free interactions. Texting 'sorry' is not as hard as saying 'sorry'. It is one thing to have the courage to ask someone on a date face-to-face (with or without a tinfoil sword and pirate outfit). It's another to let Tinder do the background checks. Clicking a box to support a cause online is not the same thing as getting up early in the rain to go on a march. What is lost in these online actions is the vulnerability and risk of putting ourselves out there; if there is no effort or cost in what we do, then there is also no reward when we succeed, and no lesson when we fail.

Social media lets us present our edited and perfect selves to the world, and that often means that we are less fully engaged in the here and now. In this one-sided interaction, something often gets lost. In a recent survey, 89 per cent of Americans admitted they took out a phone at their last social encounter, and 82 per cent said that they felt the conversation deteriorated after they did so. We are not going to get rid of our miraculous phones anytime soon, nor would most of us want to. Tough Mudder communities couldn't begin to exist without social media connections, but it's the event itself that makes those bonds meaningful. It serves as a reminder that Instagramming friends is not generally as enjoyable as seeing them – or rolling around in the mud with them – and that social people (which is all of us) sometimes forget how to be social.

The *New York Times* op-ed columnist David Brooks set out the consequences of some of our digital habits very clearly in his 2011 book *The Social Animal*. 'Decades ago, people typically told pollsters that they had four or five close friends, people to whom they could tell everything,' Brooks observed. 'Now the common answer is two or three . . . At the same time, social trust has declined. Surveys ask, "Generally speaking, would you say that most people can be trusted or that you can't be too careful in dealing with people?" In the early 1960s, significant majorities said that people can generally be trusted. But in the 1990s the distrusters had a 20-percentage-point margin over the trusters, and those margins have increased in the years since.' If we take the extra risk of interacting with people in the real world, as opposed to online, we rebuild that trust.

If Homo sapiens were in a zoo, the crate would be marked in big bold letters: DO NOT HOUSE IN ISOLATION. But the way we live and work often seems to run counter to that instruction. I was recently approached by some researchers from Harvard Divinity School working on a project called How We Gather, which was looking at the decline in communal activity in relation to the decline of religion (and also such social constructs as clubs, societies and trade unions). They wanted me to talk about the tribal aspects of Tough Mudder, the ways it brought people of different ages and backgrounds together. How We Gather was looking at a new type of business that was emerging to fill the part of people's lives that religion once satisfied. It suggests that while young people are often not looking for trad-itional faith communities, they are still very much looking for some of the benefits – togetherness, belonging, meaning – those communities once provided.

Groups centred on health and fitness are a big part of that new sense of How We Gather. Companies like CrossFit and SoulCycle inspire togetherness and offer a philosophy to their users, one of mutual emotional support and shared fitness goals.

The How We Gather researchers saw Tough Mudder as a wayward cousin to those groups. I like to think of us in that way too: different branches of the same family. Like us, CrossFit and SoulCycle are in the business of changing lives through physical challenges. And the comparison with faith is not completely fanciful – as anyone who wanders for the first time into a SoulCycle session will know. This is no ordinary spin class. It's a journey, mostly for women, led by inspirational instructors by candlelight. As the How We Gather researchers note, 'Every week, fifty thousand riders are rejuvenated by inspiring words and liturgy-like music playlists that give meaning to their workout . . .'

It would be fair to say Tough Mudder aims to offer a much more down-to-earth kind of inspiration – our playlists run from Oasis to the White Stripes to Drake and all beats in between – but, I think, the effects can be no less transformational. And they are catching.

Back in 2012 I received a job application from Marc Ackerman for the position of junior lawyer. Marc was clearly overqualified. He had spent twenty years working for prestigious New York law firms, of late as a senior partner. He had been a litigator focusing on sports – his clients included the National Football League, the National Hockey League, ESPN and the International Olympic Committee. Guy and I met him to ask a single question. Why on earth was he applying for a junior legal role with Tough Mudder?

Marc's answer was interesting. He said that despite his success as a lawyer, in recent years and particularly since the financial crash, he'd lost a bit of faith in what he did. A squeeze on costs had proved to him how the partnership ethos he had enjoyed was quite fragile, and some self-serving behaviour of colleagues when the going got tough made him feel disillusioned. He had been looking around, he said, for something more fulfilling to do with his working life. At around this point, Marc told us, a friend mentioned something about Tough Mudder, how it was like a whole new type of sport. And so he had looked up our website and liked what he saw and applied for the only lawyer job going. If there wasn't a fit, he thought, at least he gave himself a chance to meet a potential new (and different) client.

We told Marc that obviously we couldn't begin to match his previous salary. That we were not about to be the NFL or ESPN of fitness – at least not any time soon. He said that didn't matter, so we worked out a deal and a role, and Marc remains with us as our general counsel and all-round voice of reason.

He says now – and not just to me – that he has never regretted the change for an instant. That deal was sealed for him at one of the first Tough Mudder events he went to. He wanted to test his faith, he recalls, so he came along in civilian clothes and walked the course without announcing he worked for the company. At one point, Marc came across a huddle of Mudders in between obstacles. It was a very cold day, and they were wet through, covered in mud, shivering and waiting for a friend who was taking a breather. 'I went up to this group,' Marc recalls, 'and asked them, "How's it going?" They looked like some of the wettest and coldest people I'd ever seen. One of them looked at me, and I'll never forget it, and said with a big grin, "This is honestly the greatest experience of my life – it is so different from anything I've ever done." The others all agreed and when their friend recovered they set off sliding up the hill.'

I don't think the experience that Marc describes is at all unusual at our events. People take up the challenge for a thousand different reasons – because a friend has convinced them or for charity. To set themselves a fitness goal, or perhaps to overcome some life change, a breakup or a bereavement or a divorce. To prove to themselves that they can still do it, at twenty-five or fifty-five, or to show for the first time what they are capable of. But whatever the motivations, almost everyone I would say becomes at least a little bit infected with the spirit that Marc remembers.

Some of that has to do with the overcoming of obstacles. A lot more of it is probably because, as Marc's exhausted participant pointed out, this is something very different from the general run or rat race of their lives. The stories of the Mudder legends in this book back up that idea – but I believe almost all our two million headband-wearing tribe have similar stories to share. Many of them take the opportunities provided by Facebook and other social media to do just that.

Are there typical characteristics of these stories?

Each of our communities across the world has individuals who take it upon themselves to keep the tribe together, to welcome new members, and to share Mudder-related information and gossip. These notable Givers, in Adam Grant's terms, emerge spontaneously; they do it just because they believe in doing it.

Chris James, who has become a well-known figure in our UK community, is one of those online Givers, answering queries, taking the time to spread the word, occasionally giving us a bit of honest feedback. In some ways, his own Tough Mudder tale is emblematic of a lot of what we are about. Chris runs his own IT design consultancy from home. He's a natural leader – he's run martial arts groups all his adult life – but increasingly he found that, working from home, he was spending more time on his laptop than with other people. He ran his first Tough Mudder in 2012 with some friends, to counter this 'mud-life crisis' and was converted.

Chris has now, he thinks, completed more laps of the course than anyone in Europe (he runs as many UK events as he can, and with a group of friends he routinely completes three laps a weekend, two on Saturday, one on Sunday). For a while, for charity, his group carried a two-hundred-pound mannequin around the course, of the kind used by firemen to practise rescue. Chris is forty-eight now. He started originally for the physical challenge but quickly, he says, 'the camaraderie thing kicked in'.

'I met a great guy called Matt on my first Tough Mudder and we kept in touch on social media,' he recalls. 'Matt asked if I fancied doing the Scotland event. I'm like, I don't know how I'm going to get there. He says, you can jump in the car with me. I said, well, where are we going to stay? He goes, my mate Ben's got a house, so we can stay there. So we jumped in the car on a Friday night, we drove to Scotland, arrived at his mate's house at eleven p.m. I didn't know him from Adam but he'd set me up a bed. We went and did Tough Mudder in the morning and Ben came with us, and in the evening we went out for a few beers and a laugh.

'Then on Sunday me and Matt ran again. I remember we were on the top of Everest, feeling a bit groggy from the night before. There was this guy waiting to run, and I'll never forget looking at him. Let's just say he was a bit out of shape; he'd probably been a rugby player or something where he had built a lot of muscle. He was an extraordinarily big unit.

'I'm looking at Matt and we both knew: this guy is coming for us. We're both about twelve stone I guess, and this guy was getting close to twice that on his own. He charged at us and thundered up the slope. I don't know how, but somehow I got hold of his arm and Matt got hold of the other arm and he was dangling. Another bloke saw what was happening, dived on my back and grabbed on, and a woman stepped in to help. The four of us wouldn't let him go. I remember at one point I dropped his arm and grabbed his thigh, which I could hardly get my arms around. And after a long struggle we somehow got him up. And when we did, this huge bloke just burst into tears. He was hugging me and he goes, "You've changed my life. I'm going to come back next year. I know I'm a fat bastard but I'm going to change." And we both just started laughing. It was hilarious. And I thought, *This is what this is about.* Just running up a wooden slope, but there is that human touch point. You don't get held up that much in life, but it's an important thing.'

It is. It's obviously a small event in the scheme of things, but when you run at Everest you have to do so in the belief that a random stranger's hand will catch you, and if that hand isn't there you may face-plant onto the slope and hurt yourself. That hand is symbolic, but also very real. Likewise, at Berlin Wall, you can run at it as hard as you like, but you are unlikely to get over without a lift or a push or a heave from someone you have likely never met.

For a lot of reasons – some of them entirely understandable in different contexts – we don't have that many chances to be in physical contact with other human beings from all walks of life. I think we miss it.

That sense of your own body as part of a wider body of humanity is crucial to who we are. It's one of the reasons why we love festivals.

It motivates us to play contact sports or to get lost in crowds. And it's one of the reasons why people love Tough Mudder.

Physical intimacy is about trust and risk and vulnerability; in the right context – being heaved over a wall or dragged from an ice bath – it deepens that sense of mutual respect and friendship. Chris James had another eureka moment, again at Everest. 'There was a very athletic young woman I was trying to help, with very tight shorts on, and my wife was down in the crowd watching,' he says of an archetypal Tough Mudder dilemma. 'I was being the perfect gentleman and trying to pull her up in a dignified way but it wasn't working. And then I heard my wife yell "Grab her arse!" and the woman I was helping suggested the same – and she got over and again we had a laugh about it. And of course at Tough Mudder people are grabbing people all over the place – in an innocent way – and rolling around in mud. There is something very raw and human about it. A coming together in adversity.'

Physical connectedness not only builds social bonds but also, all the research suggests, makes us smarter and healthier and probably richer. Clicking on a Facebook page or liking a tweet isn't enough to create that capital. What matters is not passive spectating but active and involved joining in.

The Internet can be a brilliant tool for generating connections with people who might share our values or interests, but the connections only have demonstrably beneficial effects when they are backed up by face-to-face contact, not relied on as an alternative reality. Amelia Boone, our World's Toughest heroine, emphasizes that point about the 'tightness' of the online Mudder community that is the result of the constant 'actively involved membership' that comes with running and preparing for events and sharing stories about them. She loves the way that the community crosses social and other boundaries. 'A lot of the people I have met through Tough Mudder I have on the surface not much in common with in everyday life,' she says. 'We come from such different backgrounds and do such different things. But you put us out on a course and we share such a common bond out there that afterwards we talk to each other or text or Facebook all the time. Most lawyers tend to mix with lawyers. Through Tough Mudder I have friends who are plumbers or physiotherapists, doctors, mechanics or soldiers.'

This experience is not unusual. Once I watched a bloke in a 7 series BMW drive up and park next to a guy in a battered Ford 250 before an event. They got out and fell into animated backslapping. I assumed they were old friends, but when I got to talking with them it turned out they had never met before. One was a city banker, the other a part-time carpenter. They were desperate as soon as they arrived to share stories about previous events and anticipate the obstacles at this one. They no doubt had very different lives, but this weekend they had a shared identity.

We are constantly looking for ways to deepen those ties that bind, to strengthen the community and what it stands for. I've looked at the possibility of doing a national Mudder day with headband wearers invited to do random acts of Mudderness and be kind to people in their neighbourhoods – fetching the groceries for an elderly neighbour or helping carry bags up the stairs at the train station or whatever.

And deepening relationships within the tribe is, of course, also the motivation behind our new gym project, Tough Mudder Bootcamp, which will give Mudders and their friends the chance to experience that camaraderie year round and not just at events. In researching that idea, I met a man who runs another gym brand. He told me, by way of introduction: 'I take people and build machines.' I replied: 'But what if I don't want to be a machine? What if I want to just be in slightly better shape and get to see my friends?' The gym owner looked at me like I was insane.

With Tough Mudder Bootcamp we will not be aiming to build machines. It will be a space where Mudders can do a fitness session but also have a drink together. In my most sentimental moments I imagine that it will ideally be somewhere, like they used to say in the theme song for the TV programme *Cheers*, 'where everybody knows your name', and where it doesn't matter what level of athlete you are or how much you can bench-press.

One of the results of our risk-averse times, perhaps, is the ways in which we have often gone from being participants – in sports, in politics, in communities – to bystanders. We are more likely to observe and criticize in 140 characters than to actively participate in life and try to change things. In terms of sports there is that depressing idea, pushed by online gambling companies, that betting on the outcome of a game is somehow just the same as being part of the action. Some of this reluctance to be involved comes down to a persistent idea in our culture that if you are not gifted or competent at something, you should leave it to people who are.

While I was at Harvard, I was surrounded by a lot of people who – kabaddi aside – seemed to have, perhaps reluctantly, taken that idea to heart. Because they were so used to being ranked at everything they did, they took a low ranking as a sign that they should probably duck out before exposing themselves to any perceived failure. There was a sense that any given activity – music, baseball, politics or whatever – involved elite skills and was best practised by the gifted or not at all. This felt like an expression of a broader social trend. A perfectionist ideal seems to have invaded all walks of life and is why people don't often even make it to the starting line of a new experience for fear they would fall at the first hurdle. With this in mind, I once made another of my 'What's Will railing about now?' arguments to my long-suffering classmates at Harvard. This one was a prepared presentation about the importance of the idea of 'sixth XV rugby'.

The argument went like this. It used to be the case in any school or at any local sports club, there were not just A and maybe B teams who played rugby, but A, B, C, D, E and maybe F teams. Given that rugby teams have fifteen players, the F team – the sixth XV at rugby – was made up of the players who were not in the top seventy-five players at that sport in their group. They were likely playing the game to a pretty low standard. But the fact was, they were still play-ing the game. And rugby requires a degree of commitment and ef-fort. It doesn't work if only thirteen people out of fifteen turn up. It involves getting muddy and sorting out gear and the possibility of getting hurt and the disappointment of defeat. But the sixth XV turned up week after week and they took on fixtures against other sixth XV rugby teams, and in some ways they got as much out of it – in terms of teamwork and friendship and enjoyment and elation and despair – as those playing in the elite levels. If we focus only on skill and performance, we forget about the huge benefits of being part of something. It is not just that you should try to be as good as you can be. It is, as Adam Grant observed, that 'success doesn't measure a human being, effort does'.

Tough Mudder tries to incorporate that idea in everything we do. To do a Tough Mudder and to enjoy a Tough Mudder, you must take your fitness seriously, but you absolutely cannot take yourself seriously. A cold beer or two at the finishing line is as much a part of the event as the headbands and the pledge and the training programmes and the obstacles.

It is, obviously, a great idea to be in good shape physically. But when that determination slips over into obsession, then it is often at the expense of other important aspects of life, like spending time with family and friends or just smelling the roses. I have to work at those balances all the time myself, and I often get it wrong. I've tended to set myself ridiculous goals and to exhaust myself with trying to do too much or getting too absorbed in things that are happening in the company. I've tried to be more balanced about being more balanced.

Like the rest of us, I'm a sucker for those 'how to be a perfect you' articles that tend to crop up around the New Year and are full of all kinds of resolutions that make you feel inadequate and examples of people who abide by them religiously that make you feel hopeless. Last year, I cut one out from the *Guardian* that seemed to me a useful antidote to that – it read like the best New Year's resolution anyone could aspire to. The article was called 'How to be a moderately successful person' and – tongue firmly in cheek – it nailed the important, neglected philosophy of being happy to be here.

It began with a shorthand spoiler about the more regular secrets on offer for transforming your life. You know the ones: get up at five a.m., practise mindfulness and time management, dress to win, set personal goals, declutter and all the rest. And it replaced them with a more workable set. 'Get up at a normal time. Let yourself go a bit. Practise obliviousness (like mindfulness, except instead of acknowledging all your thoughts and emotions, you just ignore them and go about your day until something actually goes wrong). Go places using your legs. Be confused about what quality time means.'

Above all, the writer suggested one golden rule to live by, which I'd like to think is a rule all Tough Mudders, however hard they push themselves to achieve their potential, would understand: 'Sometimes, when your in-box is screaming, your phone is beeping like a rabid R2-D2, and it feels like the sky is about to come crashing down, you have to say, "Ah, fuck it." Then, go for a bottle of wine with another moderately successful person, who is also saying "Ah, fuck it," and talk about fun stuff like books and films and sex. Apply the "Ah, fuck it" rule and you can't go too far wrong.'

We are all sometimes guilty of taking life more seriously than it needs to be taken and forgetting that AFI rule. It is in those AFI moments, when we look outwards from the stresses of our lives, new bonds and friendships are often created and deepened, and tribes begin to form and creativity happens. There is, as I hope this book and our events dramatize, nothing wrong with courage and risk taking and trying to take yourself out of your comfort zone. But if that ambition is at the expense of engaging with new things and connecting with new people, then you should probably ask yourself if you are doing it wrong.

As Woody Allen observed, 'Eighty per cent of success is turning up.' If we look for every second to be purposeful and every hour to give us personal gains, we not only forget that the best of times usually happen unplanned, we stop being Givers, with all the benefits that flow from that. Control gets you only so far: sometimes we have to just close our eyes, jump into thin air, and trust that hands will be there to catch us.

MUDDER BODIES: Gaby Martinez

There has been a lot of research done about the generation now in their twenties and thirties who are ever more connected globally but have far fewer daily interactions at a local level. Headlines suggest loneliness and depression are running at record levels, even among groups that appear by many other measures to be outwardly successful. A November 2015 Pew Research Center paper found that 'nones' are growing on the basis that when asked to tick boxes about religious organizations and affiliations, 'none' is the box they overwhelmingly tick. Generally, this generation is abandoning structured political and social organizations. Yet the human need for community, for belonging, has not gone away. Churches, sports clubs and trade unions may no longer look relevant, but people still aspire to feel part of something bigger than themselves. And the question arises: how do we address that need in new ways?

One of the things that people, young people, increasingly gather around is an idea of well-being. They have seen the junk food and workaholic lives of their parents' generation and many of them rebel against it. The trend to fitness and health is stated as the number one priority in people's lives and has grown consistently over forty years (even as lifestyles militate against it). The material culture we have grown up with does not address these needs. We don't need a bigger TV or a better car any more – TVs and cars are all great – so we spend more time thinking about how we can live happier, healthier lives. We look for dramatic experiences that might enhance them. Often, though, we approach this ambition with the same seriousness with which we have long been invited to approach work. We seem to struggle sometimes with the idea of being able to muck about and have fun and relax and play.

Bodies can become symbolic of this seriousness. We make a conscious effort to avoid promoting ideals of body types at Tough Mudder. The line that you must take your fitness seriously to complete an event but you absolutely cannot take yourself seriously runs through all our communication with the tribe. Six-packs and zero body fat are great for some, but they are not a Tough Mudder requirement. All shapes and body sizes are equally welcome on our course, and now, in our Tough Mudder Bootcamp gyms, where grit and determination and a willingness to have fun are the only mandatory attributes. Still, signing up for an event certainly tends to concentrate the mind. Twelve miles up and down muddy hills and over obstacles is not something you'd be advised to take on from a standing start. The six or nine months before it happens generally involve at least some kind of determined sofa-leaving regime. We once calculated that, on average, each person who signs up for a Tough Mudder sheds around twenty pounds of fat before they take part. If you multiply that number by our two and a half million participants, that's 50 million pounds (or 220 blue whales' worth) of blubber that we have been directly responsible for shifting. Dr Atkins, watch out.

Some people have done more to improve that statistic than others. Gaby Martinez completed a Tough Mudder in Illinois in 2013 in a T-shirt that said on the back: 'I used to weigh 330 pounds and I have just run past you.' She was just about 170 pounds lighter than

that when she received her first headband. That T-shirt commem-
orated the darkest time in Gaby's life, when she was twenty-four and
her husband, who had been unfaithful to her, left her with their
three-year-old son.

Like many of us, looking back, Gaby can't separate her weight
issues from her mental health at that time. 'That lowest point was I
was in a bad depression because I was so heavy and I was eating
because I was so depressed. I couldn't break that circle. My husband
and I had just split up and I had my little boy, and I was all alone. And
just constantly eating.'

Food had always been a problem in Gaby's life. She grew up big,
a casualty of that shift in working habits between generations. Her
mum and dad are not exercise mad but they were blue-collar physical workers, so they naturally kept weight off. Her dad worked in a
factory and was sweating from head to toe forty hours a week. Her
mum worked in a factory and as a cleaner. 'So they were both on
their feet and active, and they never had a problem with food. They
needed a lot of energy. My mum makes food that's not greasy or anything but they eat; their portions are big.'

Gaby herself trained as a laser eye specialist, which did not involve much heavy lifting. She didn't play any sports, but her big
plates of food became a habit, then an addiction: 'I didn't even know
what it was like to be hungry because there was always food in my
belly.'

She can't exactly place the moment she decided to turn things
around, but there was a voice in her head that abruptly said enough,
and that was the start. Her friends encouraged her to go to the gym,
but given the stigma about body shapes, she says that was too embar-
rassing originally: 'You can't even go to the gym when you weigh 330

pounds. Even in the gym, especially in the gym, the place you would think you would have support in trying to get fitter, people look at you funny, like you don't belong there. You want to say: "Look I'm here trying to do something about it!" It's like you can't win anywhere. So I actually started working out at home. That was my starting point.'

At the same time, she gave up buying any junk food, no rubbish. And the more she exercised the less she craved the salt and sugar. People began to tell her she had great willpower. Developing will-power became unavoidable because maintaining the change became such a big part of her life once she started to shed weight. Still, it took her a couple of years to get to the point where she did her first Tough Mudder.

That first one she did with a friend. The most recent was with her new husband and brother- and sister-in-law – she got married for the second time last summer.

Gaby's T-shirt provoked some laughter going around. Best was when she ran past a group of guys, pretty tough guys, who had slowed to a walk; when they read what was written on her T-shirt, they all laughed and told her: good job. 'It's funny,' she says, 'I don't have the upper body strength but I do have endurance, I find I can just keep going and going which is something I would never have imagined.'

In many ways, the best part of that determination is that Gaby sees it rubbing off on those around her. She has gained a few pounds since her wedding, so she is back to training and is determined to shift them. Her son, now in his teens, appreciates that effort. She fears he has her genes so she worries about him. She is proud of the fact that he will say, after her example, 'Mum, I won't eat dessert today because I've eaten dessert a couple of days this week already.'

She thinks he makes healthier decisions knowing what the effects can be.

She laughs about having become the go-to person for any of her friends looking to get in better shape. But she tells them what she has learned: that there is no magic pill, that it's about eating and exercising, drinking water not fizzy drinks. 'I just tell them you have to make the decision in your head and be tired of it, be tired of feeling that way, just make it and stick to it. After that,' she says, 'anything is possible.'

CHAPTER 8

Tough Lessons: Learning from Failure

The arrogance of success is to think that what you did yesterday will be sufficient for tomorrow.

– William Pollard

At the end of 2012 I flew back from our second event in Australia, where I had been introduced at the starting line to five thousand Aussie Mudders who, surreally, went down on one knee in my presence. The flight to New York is sixteen hours, generally with a stopover in LA. On the first part of that flight a heavy cold I had been nursing developed into full-blown pneumonia. I had to leave the plane and, unsure where to go, holed up in an airport hotel to try to sleep it off. It was the first time for several months that I stopped working a back-to-back schedule, and as soon as I did, I collapsed.

Creating Tough Mudder and trying to help it grow – at the same time making constant operational decisions, not to mention deploying teams to build events on three continents and trying to set up robust internal systems – had meant an intense workload. That overnight stay in the LA airport hotel extended to a few days and then a week. I felt too ill to get to A & E, just occasionally summoning the energy to Skype Katie to let her know I was still there but was, honestly, about to head home. In the previous weeks I'd been travelling so much from one event to the next that I never seemed to be on the same time zone as friends and family. I felt suddenly alone. Everyone was worried about me and to be honest, though it's not really in my character, I was a bit worried about me as well. I remember thinking, on a loop: *I have to get home.* And then, *I can't leave the hotel because I don't have the strength to pick up my suitcase.*

This went on for a few more days, but eventually I did work up that strength and got back to New York. However, now well behind with all our best-laid plans and delivery goals, and with a new season's events to get control of, I plunged straight back into work. I had a sense that I couldn't slow down, or step away, because too much depended on me. We had gone from nothing to a fifty-million-dollar business in a very short time, and the last thing I wanted was for it all to come crashing down. The court case with Mr Mouse had taken more out of me than I thought, and there were a hundred other pressing anxieties and responsibilities. And then the thing that I had dreaded since we had started the business happened. In April, a young man, twenty-eight years old, died at the Walk the Plank obstacle in our event at Gerrardstown, West Virginia.

We had known deep down that statistically it had been bound to happen. We knew, for example, that one in sixty thousand competitors dies during a triathlon, and by 2013 we'd had well over a million participants complete our twelve miles – but it did not change the fact for any of us that a young man had lost his life. As founder of the company, with all the emotional investment that involved, it took me a long time to process the fact, and it inevitably cast a cloud over the whole company that summer.

One result of that and many other insistent concerns was that I wasn't sleeping well and routinely forced myself to work beyond my normal endurance levels. Though I talked a lot about the importance of balance, pushing myself – and others – harder and harder had started to become a kind of addiction as well as a point of honour: it was what Tough Mudder was all about, right? We kept going. And then we went some more. It was a habit I had practised to a degree throughout my twenties, particularly at the Foreign Office, where work-aholism was pretty much assumed: the terrorists never stopped so how could we? It began to creep into everything I did. I remember Alex Patterson persuading me to take an afternoon to go surfing one Saturday out in the Rockaways. There were some big waves and everyone was pretty tired in the swell after about twenty minutes. I stayed out in the waves on my own for two or three more hours. When I got to shore, people were asking, 'Aren't you exhausted?' I was like, 'You know, I am always exhausted.' Some months later, I did the Help for Heroes hundred-mile bike ride overnight. I hadn't done any training at all for it, just got on the bike and went through it without a break. People say that you are running on adrenaline at those times but I think it's more just a stubborn refusal to stop because of all the problems stopping implies you have – not least of which is the acknowledgement that your current level of effort is not sustainable. TMHQ had long been a family, but increasingly that was at the expense of any life outside the company. That summer I started wearing a beard because I would always need to hide at least one boil on my face.

The longer you push yourself in that way, the more you come to realize that brute resilience on its own will carry you for only so long. Work must be balanced by proper rest and perspective – and given purpose by a sense of fun. The casualty, in the absence of these factors, is your good judgement. I think up until then I had been pretty effective at thinking strategically about the growth of the business. I had a clear sense of Tough Mudder priorities at different stages of development. In the first two years, it was all about trying to deliver the events themselves seamlessly and safely. We hired some people with deep experience of event operations – people who had done logistics for Grand Slam tennis tournaments and rock festivals, and several who had been involved in the London Olympics – and that capacity improved substantially.

We had, too, worked hard on our marketing and our innovation, driving growth, adding ever more Tough Mudder events, making the business international. We worked tirelessly to create a culture of excellence, forever drilling down into problems, asking all the whys. Despite all this we were inevitably making up some strategies on the hoof, and the questions kept coming: which parts of these processes shall we do ourselves and which should we farm out? How do we interact with our providers, our contractors, our venues? Should we buy land and have permanent sites? Our small team was putting on an event for many thousands of people in sixty places around the world, sometimes four times in one weekend. We were setting up military-style camps outside a city, taking on the enormous expense of developing obstacles and of safety and insurance, and trying to build an organization that could cope with that and at the same time remain true to our values. Cracks inevitably formed.

In October 2013, when we opened our bookings for the year ahead, it quickly became clear that they were markedly down on budgeted projections. It was the first time this had happened since we launched. The bookings were not down across the board, and not in all territories – Britain and Australia were performing well – but they had dipped significantly for certain events in the United States. To begin with we weren't sure how to react. Was this a blip or was it a trend? Most concerning was that our repeat business, consistently about a third of all bookings and the lifeblood of the company and the tribe, seemed to be falling significantly behind our projections. But with an increasing number of events and new initiatives and a growing workforce, costs were going in the other direction.

I had been waiting for this moment and these numbers: one of the first ideas I had taken to heart when I started Tough Mudder was Andrew Grove's famous mantra at Intel that in business 'only the paranoid survive'. I knew that growth curves never went only one way. It was a lesson also hard learned in my time at the Foreign Office, where a healthy degree of short-term paranoia, along with a clear faith in long-term strategy, was sometimes literally a matter of life and death. However much you tell yourself to expect the worst, though, success can breed a sense of invincibility. And if you are not careful, that belief can also start to define you.

That belief had certainly taken root in some corners of TMHQ. So the sudden sense not of imminent crisis but of things not growing merrily year after year as they had done changed the atmosphere around the company. A few people, both inside and outside, took it as a cue to question our future. Having for three years been the serial disrupter of the endurance fitness world we were now faced with a few more competitors, some trying to be as nimble as we had been in the beginning. And as with any new business that matures, a little of our novelty had worn off.

That summer, we had hired our 150th employee, and revenue reached ninety million dollars. I sent a company letter round that described this expansion as being like that of a boa constrictor that has recently swallowed a large mammal. 'If we process this all correctly,' I wrote, 'we are going to be well set for a long time – but the scope for indigestion is also very high.'

That latter prophecy proved true. As all entrepreneurs learn sooner or later, growth may be the goal of your business, but it is also its potentially fatal flaw. The transition from start-up to something with a sustainable life of its own – the infamous journey from good to great – is invariably a painful one. The skills and character that you need to make the first leap into the unknown are not the same resources you need to create something stable enough to withstand inevitable reverses of market and fortune. These strains showed for me as I tried to make that transition from founder to leader. The entrepreneurial mind-set encourages you to fix things on your own – that self-reliance is the answer. I was always well aware of that voice, and its limitations. I knew the importance of sharing responsibility. But in extreme situations, the voice could be insistent.

I took some comfort from the knowledge that no one is exempt from this reality. It was true for Steve Jobs, as he discovered after getting forced out of Apple in 1985, and then watching the company's decline to near bankruptcy through the Apple Newton disasters of the early 1990s. It was true for Phil Knight at Nike, which enjoyed explosive growth in its first years, only to be eclipsed by Reebok in the mid-1980s. Knight's response was to 'Just do it' – to both intensify and diversify the brand, proving wrong the headline writers who were already creating obituaries for his company. Elon Musk's stellar career, meanwhile, has been a series of near-death experiences that resulted from trying to go as far as possible as fast as possible. Musk came close to losing all of the fortune that he had made from PayPal when his first three rocket launches at SpaceX exploded, simultaneously destroying his investors' confidence. He stuck with his beliefs, though, and found the solutions that led to NASA investing $1.6 billion in his company.

That's the price of experience. I have talked a lot in this book about resilience, about grit. It is a relatively easy thing to be resilient and gritty, to work punishing hours and to put in that extra effort in life when all you can see is sunlit improvement. The real test of character, though, comes when you try to maintain that determination and drive in the face of serious storms. I was not naive enough to imagine that Tough Mudder, like any start-up that makes money, had not benefited from a great deal of luck at the outset, for offering the right experience at just the right time. If, for example, advertising through Facebook had been priced in 2010 as it was priced in 2014, we would never have got off the ground. But luck will only ever take you so far. People talk about companies having growing pains, and there is truth in that idea, but the pains are not the benign discomforts that the phrase suggests. They put at risk everything that you have worked for.

I had prided myself, and our start-up team, on four virtues, each of which I've explored in this book: the people we hired, the culture we created, the innovation we practised and the leadership we demonstrated. At the beginning of 2014 it was becoming evident that we were coming up short in all four areas. We had hired some of the wrong people, the culture was losing its focus as a result, we had stopped doing new things as effectively or memorably, and our leadership, including my own, was less coherent than it had been. As anyone who runs a business will tell you, it is rarely one thing that causes a dip in fortunes, but an accumulation of different, related things. And though these things appear to come at you suddenly and all at once, they are generally rooted in missteps and wrong decisions – and lack of balance and overwork – made in the past.

One of my initial responses to those cracks was to hire a layer of experienced senior managers across the business from the corporate world who I believed could think strategically, to take some of the burden off myself and give me space to breathe. All of these people were highly qualified, maybe eight or nine of them, attracted by the prospect of doing something different and strapping themselves in to a high-octane start-up. To persuade some of them to join us we gave out some fancy titles: a Chief People Officer, a Chief Concept Officer. What I discovered, however, was that when the going got tough – and in the absence of some of the insulating certainties they had been used to in a larger corporation – some of these chiefs tended to retreat into their comfort zone, which was for analysis rather than hands-on intervention. They became defensive and risk averse. They would 'offer inputs' rather than getting urgent stuff done, spend a lot of time and energy justifying inaction. Some of those with a management consultant background would argue to me that they were bringing process and structure to the business, but too often the reality was that they were making us prematurely bureaucratic and overly consensual. I had, in retrospect, deviated from what I had learned to be true, that understanding of our values was the key criterion in the team; all the corporate experience in the world was no substitute for that. (I'm all for 'buy in' as far as it goes, but there is, too, an important lesson to be learned for young businesses from Richard Branson's mantra: 'Screw it, let's do it.')

To take one example, we desperately needed the website updating so that we could create a more fluent experience for new Mudders. I gave one of our chiefs responsibility for the change. He responded by producing a two-hundred-page PowerPoint document about all the ways it could be done. It took me eight hours just to go through the endless slides about the fors and againsts of the tweaks he was suggesting, which concluded with an outline of the potential risk to the business of making any change at all. At the end of it I said to him: 'Why didn't you just trial your best idea and then revise it until it worked?'

Elsewhere, despite our Ninja recruiting strategies, in an effort to expand our capacity quickly we found that we had hired people in key positions who didn't intuitively understand the culture. Because in the beginning we were all so hands-on with every aspect of the business, the nuances of our culture didn't have to be explained; we had all grown up with them. As we hired more experienced people, who had done their time in very different cultures, some of the more intangible spirit of those tribal values was harder to communicate. There were tensions, too, between our original hires, who didn't need telling about our values, and those who didn't quite get it. The culture of any company is hard to define exactly, until you come up against people who don't understand it. By 2014, I found that I was starting to have to explain myself and my instincts for Tough Mudder more and more often in meetings.

Again, a representative example sticks in my mind. I've mentioned how we have spent a lot of time getting the names and branding language right to emphasize an irreverent attitude. It's a tone of voice (never quite in earnest, 'I do not whine – kids whine') that the tribe knows well and understands. In 2014, we were developing the idea that gave special privileges to our returning Mudders. One was an exclusive obstacle that would allow them to bypass the Electro-shock Therapy if they chose to. I wanted to signify this by calling the returning Mudders 'Repeat Offenders'. In a meeting, one of our re-cently hired chiefs on the marketing team told me extremely bluntly: no way.

I wondered why?

'You are making a bad joke out of domestic violence,' she said.

I am?

'Can't you see that calling people "repeat offenders" makes you sound like you sympathize with violent criminals and wife-beaters? You can't do that.'

I didn't know whether to be more surprised by the fact of this heartfelt outburst of political correctness or its implications for what my colleague appeared to think about my character. In the large company she had come from, she had learned, I guess, to be hyper-aware that a significant marketing priority was to avoid any poten-tial for causing offence. That was undoubtedly useful when you were dealing with the broadest possible global demographic and needed a tone that traded in simplistic family values. But we were in a busi-ness that prided itself on understanding exactly how our Tough Mudder tribe spoke, and how it expected to be spoken to. Nothing about our messaging was to be taken quite in earnest. I had no doubt they would take the (small) joke in the spirit it was intended.

Still, I compromised. We eventually settled on a different for-mula, one that I also liked (and that the marketing chief also disliked because of its 'mercenary subtext'), which became the beginning of our Legionnaire programme. At the same time, I made a mental note that we were in danger of drifting badly off message in our marketing department. We wanted people who spoke their minds. I was more than happy to have strong debates about small details; but I also needed to feel that there were certain shared assumptions of what we were about. I felt that if this highly qualified person could be so wrong about my intentions in the tone of that small thing, she would likely be slightly wrong about the tone of everything.

There were a hundred other similar issues that collectively began to change how we operated. As we scaled up we needed to become more 'professional' by necessity, but that couldn't be at the expense of our values. When we were a smaller company there was no room for us to get attached to different pieces of work or systems or obstacles. The idea was that you produced something as good as you could make it and then it belonged to everybody and could be refined and reexamined by whoever had the best ideas.

Now, though, people were saying, 'I have designed this system and it works; let's not change it.' Or new projects – from changes in event formats to new media opportunities – were blocked internally because they were 'too much of a risk', words that I didn't want to hear. 'Give me an exact idea of that risk,' I would say, 'or tell me how the risk can be decreased and how much that will cost, but don't shut things down because they don't conform to ways that we are already doing things.'

We had also stopped paying enough attention to a few of the things that had got us to where we were. The pressure simply to deliver the growing number of events left us little time for broader personal development; the case study events were more sporadic. We got together less as a team. And there was, because of all these habits, something of a minor breakdown in that collaborative spirit that had fuelled our early I've-got-your-back ethos. The original team grew a little disillusioned by the fact that more recent arrivals didn't seem to buy into the collective spirit. That breakdown was compounded by a sense of panic in some quarters about the sudden decline in bookings.

In a 'tribal' business, such changes in tone and practice are quickly felt beyond the office. One of the advantages about having a committed Mudder community that talks among itself nonstop is that we soon get to know of small changes in collective mood. Some of the Mudder community leaders picked up on the problems we were starting to have. They saw it out on the course itself. Jim Campbell, who recently became the first Mudder to complete a hundred events, recalls how in 2014 the company that he had come to know and love from the beginning seemed to be losing a bit of its mojo for the first time.

'It had a stumbling year,' Campbell says now. 'The obstacles themselves seemed for the first time a bit predictable. And people started to talk; they'd say, "Yeah, they are cutting corners." It started to look more like a commercial thing and therefore a lot less like Tough Mudder. The company had done more than enough up to that point for people like me to keep the faith, though,' Campbell argues, 'so I responded to this criticism in the community: "Hey you know it is just a bad year. And they are going to get it back up." But people were saying, "Screw this, there are plenty of other events to choose from. Tough Mudder has to worry about keeping my attention here."'

It was as much a coincidence of timing as anything, but I couldn't help thinking that part of this perceived loss of purpose and authenticity had to do with the physical relocation of the office. In 2013, we moved from our rough-and-ready start-up space in DUMBO, which had been divided between two sites, to seventy thousand square feet of prime office space in the commercial heart of Brooklyn's Metro-Tech. As a business, we were probably ready for the upshift, but I couldn't help feeling it had added a bit more of a corporate edge to how some people started to carry themselves. We took over the new office in November 2013, in high Mudder excitement, seventy of us donning headbands and charging in through the lobby en masse, somewhat to the alarm of security. But I feared that attitude had started to wane not long after we arrived.

I was reminded of a scene in the film *Wayne's World*, in which Wayne and Garth hit the big time with the TV show they have been making in Wayne's basement. To make themselves feel comfortable in the new professional studio they are given, they try to re-create an exact replica of that basement, just as it was – but a little bit of the old pioneer spirit is inevitably lost. I think all start-ups that are successful experience some of that loss-of-innocence feeling when the need to scale means that things begin to become more routine.

This feeling was compounded by the fact that by the time we relocated, I was leading the company without my co-founder, my old friend from school, Guy Livingstone. Guy agreeing to join was the first step in my believing that the company was for real and our adventures at Tough Mudder were nearly all shared.

Guy had a manic work ethic and for two and a half years at Tough Mudder he was, like me, a man possessed. His energy and range of abilities were exactly what Tough Mudder needed: he was equally at home in a formal meeting one minute, terrier-like in negotiations with suppliers the next, and then happy to be putting up obstacles at three in the morning in muddy fields. He was a close confidant for me and a source of good sense. I doubt, for example, that we would have got through the lawsuit with Mr Mouse had it not been for Guy helping to manage that and keep a sense of perspective.

That intense start-up energy does not suit itself to the longer haul. As the company grew, Guy's role became necessarily less hands-on, and he seemed to miss some of the former intensity. Both of us could see this happening, and we discussed how we should address it. Reluctantly, given what we had been through together, we agreed that Guy should leave his day-to-day involvement in Tough Mudder, while retaining his significant shareholding. We parted company amicably in the summer of 2013.

Guy's departure was inevitable in hindsight, but in the short term it meant that I had lost a partner. We had shared some of the duties of communicating with the Tough Mudder tribe and the TMHQ team. By the beginning of 2014, when more numbers were coming in and still not quite adding up, that communication seemed to have narrowed to answering a single question, one that suddenly followed me around every media interview and crept into every company meeting. It was a version of the same question that had been asked of Steve Jobs and Elon Musk and Phil Knight and every other entrepreneur at some point. 'What if Tough Mudder is a fad, Will? What if it's already had its moment?'

The persistence of that question – and its subtext, 'What if you've failed, Will?' – consumed my thinking. I'd studied the experiences of enough entrepreneurs to know that how you reacted after the first spike of growth determined whether you would sink or swim for the wider ocean. I certainly wasn't about to give up on what we had built, so I took a breath and started swimming.

When you think about it, I told myself and those around me,

every single business idea is a fad. Nothing stays the same, as the market and the environment in which you operate are always shifting. The priorities you face at the beginning are not those you will face after three years, let alone five or ten. I was anxious about how best to change, but confident that we would.

That confidence was heartfelt. However much I interrogated it, my central belief remained secure that the things Tough Mudder was offering – a fitness goal, a tribal community, a real-life challenge – were not going to lose their appeal any time soon. But what was increasingly clear was that we had to find some new ways of offering them. We couldn't simply rely on adding more events.

I knew I needed some help in giving the company a broader base and more diversified revenue – an executive team that could help shape where we were going and give me more time and space to make the transformation. But I also knew that I couldn't simply repeat the error of hiring people with quite similar corporate experience who did not share all our values. A friend and mentor, Strauss Zelnick, CEO of the games publisher Take-Two Interactive (which owns Grand Theft Auto among others), suggested that perhaps one thing I needed was someone who had learned this price of experience himself and lived to tell the tale. He introduced me to Adam Slutsky. Adam had been a great success in the 1990s dot-com years. He had been instrumental in creating Moviefone, the original online movie ticketing service, which he took from start-up to IPO to an eventual $550 million takeover by AOL. When he first came on board at the end of 2013 he was leaving a CEO role at Mimeo.com.

Adam and I are very different. His instinct is to go first for detail and short-term issues, mine to see bigger pictures. He likes to talk his way to solutions; I like some time to analyse options. But we are similarly driven by an entrepreneurial personality – a determination to keep getting over one obstacle and then the next. The timing was also good – Adam didn't want to start again from scratch, but to employ some of the lessons he had learned. I needed a reliable day-to-day handle on the business while I worked out the coordinates of where Tough Mudder was heading next.

In the first instance, we separated out the problems. Adam examined our costs, identified some areas for immediate savings, and worked – with some trial and error – to make our 'back office' less top-heavy. He relied enormously on one of the chiefs I had brought in, Don Baxter, who had been a wise and hugely positive COO and now CFO, but otherwise we agreed that we had 'too many chiefs', so we made the never-easy decision of removing most of that layer of strategic management that was proving so hard to integrate into the culture. This involved most of the repeat-offending marketing department, and eventually the entire layer of PowerPoint-ing chiefs.

Determined not to make the same mistakes, we hired a new marketing director, Jerome Hiquet, who was working with a different tribe at the tourism giant Club Med. I had always tried to put candidates through some hard interviews, but given our recent success rate, I was more paranoid than usual about getting this wrong. Jerome still reminds me how we put him through eleven interviews – the last one over a Tough Mudder course, in some hastily borrowed and ill-fitting gear – before he got the job. Once in place, though, he hit the ground running. Jerome helped me to implement what I could already see: that we needed to think of Tough Mudder as much as a media company as an events company. That our great strength lay in the tribe itself, the faith it showed in us, and the loyalty it demonstrated to the Tough Mudder spirit. We went back to our mission statement and worked on ways to deepen and extend our relationship with the tribe by making the experience ever more available to them, talking to them in different ways and over different channels.

To this end, we started to live stream the event from the course (and overnight millions of Mudders old and new were tuning in). We had long thought about how to do TV without compromising the authenticity of Tough Mudder. Jerome helped us to develop a relationship with CBS that involved two strands – a documentary-style series about World's Toughest Mudder, presenting it as the ultimate physical challenge, and a series (on the CW network) that depicted some of the superhuman stories of everyday Mudder legends. We have subsequently deepened that relationship by creating TMX, a one-mile Tough Mudder that pits speed against strength, and will be televised on Saturday afternoons in 2017.

While we were working on this shift to other media, the key problem we needed to address was the fall-off in repeat business: the fact that Mudders were doing one event and then not coming back. The blip in fortunes I had identified in October 2013 had become a trend by early 2014, and one that, at the time, offered an existential threat to the business if not quickly reversed.

We created a double strategy to keep Mudders coming back. It was clear that we needed to streamline our operations to focus a lot more of our resources on obstacle innovation – our unique selling point. With Nolan Kombol's expanded team we created what was effectively a whole new event in 2014, updating and replacing obstacles, ready to roll out in 2015. We celebrated by making the launch of the new obstacles themselves an annual landmark.

To reinforce that innovative spirit and to extend the reach of Tough Mudder we also developed a series of formats that would appeal to other demographics without diluting the authenticity of the original – Tough Mudder Half (without ice or electricity), TM5K, Toughest Mudder. And we worked to try to enhance the experience for returning Mudders. In thinking about how to reward this ongoing loyalty I had what I believed to be a simple but effective idea, which I planned to announce at our annual retreat at the beginning of 2014.

My thought was just this: returning Mudders, though running alongside first timers, would be rewarded for their loyalty with some special features (exclusive obstacles, early booking discounts and so on) and also, at different milestones of Tough Mudder events completed, be awarded a different colour of headband as a recognition of their new status. From the beginning our legionnaires had sewn their orange headbands together to make hats – until there were too many to make that practical (or a very good look). The new headband colours – a green headband for two-time Mudders, blue for three, yellow for four to six, black for ten and so on – would create a hierarchy of Mudders, much like the belt system in martial arts. It wasn't a particularly subtle strategy, but I had no doubt it would be welcomed by the tribe. Any rite of passage demands a badge of recognition. There was something extra special about the people who took on our challenge more than once, and that needed acknowledgement. I thought that the idea was a no-brainer, but in terms of its reception within TMHQ I could hardly have been more wrong.

For our weekend away at the retreat, we always take over the same hotel in Upstate New York. It has a kind of faded sixties charm, slightly reminiscent of *The Shining*. There is a big cavernous ballroom where we do presentations and speeches and give out jokey awards. I stood up in this ballroom and made my speech, which set out some of the issues around return business, and some of the proposed solutions, climaxing in this revolutionary announcement:

'We're not just going to have orange headbands. We're going to have other colours!'

Silence.

I looked around the room and there were mainly blank – or slightly pained-looking – faces. I made the case in a bit more detail. More silence. So I invited comments. Almost everyone said the same thing.

'Will, you know we only have orange headbands!'

'Orange is our brand; you'd just be diluting it!'

I was stunned. In some ways those responses might have sounded like a good thing: they showed how passionate the team was about preserving the authenticity of our trademarks. But I also was sure they were short-sighted. I was angry with myself for not having gauged this mood in advance and as a result had a sense of personal failure that my thinking was not more closely attuned to that of the team. Since the beginning, I had not only tried to drill into the company the importance of pride in things like our headband, but moreover, I believed, the idea that changing realities always required changing responses. Innovation was not an option for us. It was a given. Nothing could ever be set in stone. The attitude towards the headbands demonstrated exactly the dangers in a business of an ingrained determination to do the same thing even if the same thing is not proving enough. For a moment, standing in that room, being told that I could not alter what I had created, I glimpsed how Dr Frankenstein must have felt.

The other reason that this came as a surprise to me was that I am generally the first to veto ideas that go against our core values. There was, at one point, for example, much enthusiasm for a Tough Mudder video game, which I rejected because it sent a directly contrary message to the one we were trying to promote: of switching off phones for an afternoon and committing to getting involved in real-world challenges. There was a big difference between a TV show that tells the stories of Tough Mudder and communicates our mission and values and a computer game that promotes inactivity, disconnection and living by proxy. Again, the headbands were a different matter. They did nothing that compromised our culture – in fact they enhanced it by offering a further reward for the doggedness and keep-on-keeping-on grit of the tribe.

The TMHQ team mostly remained unconvinced, but they grudgingly agreed to at least test the idea. We promoted it first at our event that year in Sydney. Within twenty-four hours of the event we were up a clear 10 per cent on repeat bookings. By 2015 – with other innovations in obstacle design and format creation and marketing strategy also kicking in – we went from 20 per cent of Mudders booking to come back to more than 40 per cent. That figure now stands at over half of all our Tough Mudders repeat offending. The return rate is such that in 2016 we introduced 25x and 50x headbands. This shift not only helped to turn around the financial picture, it proved that the sense of the novelty of the event wearing off could be transformed. It did this not only in the minds of our legionnaires, but also – crucially – within the company. Like anyone else, I don't ever mind being proved right, but the more important lesson that I think we all came away with was that the change had been good for the company. It was a huge credit to the team that they came to embrace the shift as their own. In 2016, our year on year numbers for every single event went up, and that trend continues. It proved the point that innovation can create a constant sense of renewal. Increasingly for the tribe, as I hoped, Tough Mudder became not a one-off life experience but an annual or a monthly challenge, a habit that becomes more meaningful and enjoyable with repetition. And in my mind, the coloured headbands became emblematic of all the other changes that we made, of the importance of never standing still.

The current business is differently structured from Tough Mudder at the beginning of 2014. The changes we made in response to the challenges we faced have in many ways proved the making of Tough Mudder. We have continued to expand across the globe but have taken steps to spread the risk and the pressure on our resources by partnering with IMG to develop and deliver events in Asia and Dubai. We have worked hard on creating diverse revenue streams to continue to improve the Mudder experience itself. We have a new range of sponsors, and many new ways for Mudders to interact with us – not just live streaming and TV, but also our gym programme, which launched in 2017 and is already giving Mudders another crucial way of keeping closely in touch with tribal values in the months between events.

Our overall goal in 2014 was to make Tough Mudder more sustainable in the long term by shifting the burden of the business away from ticket sales so we could cope more readily with any future fluctuation. We are moving towards the target I set for 50 per cent of our revenue to come not from ticket sales, but from commercial partners by 2020 (in 2013, 90 per cent of our revenue was from ticket sales; in 2016, it was less than 75 per cent). This allows us above all to continue to live up to our mission statement of continuing to grow the Tough Mudder tribe, investing all the time in innovation, and never forgetting the values that we share. The sense of sustainable growth that has resulted can be felt in the restored atmosphere at TMHQ and beyond: our employee engagement levels are higher than ever. Happily, we are no longer burning people out (including me).

On the walls of TMHQ we have some posters of figures from history wearing a Tough Mudder headband. Each of the historical figures comes with a quote. A cigar-clutching Winston Churchill reminds us that 'all men make mistakes, but only wise men learn from their mistakes', while Steve Jobs, who looks suitably wise in his orange headband, makes this observation, which is aimed squarely at myself: 'I hate it when people call themselves entrepreneurs when what they're really trying to do is launch a start-up and then sell it or go public so they can cash in or move on. They are unwilling to do the work it takes to build a real company, which is the hardest work in business. That's when you really make a contribution and add to the legacy of those that went before.'

The work we did after 2014 was my response to Jobs's implicit challenge. From the beginning of 2012 there have been offers that would have allowed me to cash in on what I started. Seductive though some of those offers have been financially, I've not been tempted to take them up.

If I ask myself why, the answer goes back to that sense of mission that I outlined earlier in this book. Tough Mudder was not created to make me rich (though, like most of us, having had times in my life when I have worried about money on a personal level, not worrying about it, for myself or my family, is a much preferable alternative). But rather, the business was created to prove a point. It was made – as our office Gandhi-in-a-headband has it – to 'be the change you want to see in the world'. Part of that change was a demonstration of the importance of persevering when everyone around you is expecting you to give up or stop. We are lucky as a business that almost every weekend we have tens of thousands of examples from Mudder participants that true satisfaction comes not from winning easily but from overcoming serious setbacks in order to reach a goal. If they could keep optimistic and resourceful through adversity, then so could we.

The prospect of failure teaches us humility, but it also gives us the opportunity to not let it win. That is why I argue, when asked, that 2014 was not our year of crisis but in fact our most important year of opportunity. In a business of overcoming tough challenges, it was the rite of passage by which we came of age. We didn't underestimate it, but we got it done. It revealed a truth that I try to keep at the front of our minds as we develop our next phase. The truth is there is no finishing line when creating a company. Any business must always think of itself as an unfinished business, and all proper work is work in progress.

MUDDER MIRACLES: Ilene Boyar

While I was at Harvard I had a bad bike accident. A cab pulled out from a side road, hit me at thirty miles an hour, and drove off. By the time I landed at the kerb, I had exploded a disk in my back and done some long-term damage to my spine. A series of operations that followed involved six months of recuperation. The result of this is that I must do up to an hour's concentrated stretching each morning before I can get my back moving without too much pain and stiffness. (I tend to also use the stretching time as profitably as I can to catch up on TED talks.) It's a very minor injury compared with the pain that many people have to live with, but I mention it only to say that, if anything, it has deepened my determination to keep meeting physical challenges. It's also one of the things that makes me empathize with the thousands of extraordinary Tough Mudders who get around our event with physical difficulties of all kinds and to appreciate how that fact makes the achievement more meaningful – and enjoyable – to them when they do.

Of all the Mudders who have earned their headband in this way, one of the most extraordinary is Ilene Boyar, a native of Connecticut, who signed up for her first Tough Mudder in 2012. I have talked in this book about the life-affirming potential of doing things that take you out of your comfort zone. Ilene has never enjoyed a comfort zone at all. She was born with a rare disease called osteogenesis imperfecta, a particularly severe form of what is commonly called brittle bone syndrome. Ilene has fractured every bone in her legs at least once and one femur alone five times, which has left her in continuous chronic pain. Four times in childhood she was placed in a full body cast, for a broken back (on one occasion, on the basis that she probably couldn't do much further harm, her friends put her in a garbage bag, cast and all, and she sledded triumphantly downhill). She's broken all her fingers and some ribs and suffered more stress fractures and torn ligaments than she can begin to count. Until the age of sixteen she was mainly in a wheelchair, to avoid falling over. As she got older, though the disease affects her balance, she took the risk of walking with crutches – and then, sometimes, without them.

Ilene took part in her first Tough Mudder in 2012. After seeing a picture of Noah Galloway cheerfully carrying a log on his back on a Mudder course, with his missing arm and prosthetic leg, she contacted him on Facebook on a whim and explained how she would love to have a go at a Tough Mudder. She also explained her challenges. The approach was very much out of character for her, as 'in those days', she says, 'I didn't reach out to anyone I didn't know ever.' The following day Galloway messaged her back to tell her that she should name the time and place for the Mudder event she wanted to do, and he would get a team together that would commit to helping her get around. Ilene cried when she read that note. It was the word 'team' that set her off; she had never been part of one before.

Team Ilene, which consisted of sixteen volunteers, convened at the Florida event. Some people said that getting around the course at all would be an achievement and that Ilene should skip any obstacle that she couldn't face, but she did them all, with help from her friends, apart from Funky Monkey, which was too high off the ground for her to have support. It took the team close to twelve hours to complete the course. Ilene had never in her life walked as far and as long as she did that day.

Since then she has done many more Mudders and other obstacle events. The Team Ilene Facebook page only includes friends who have completed a whole course with her. That group now numbers 195 people. These days she posts a time and place for the next event that she wants to do, and invariably overnight a team has signed up to support her. 'I'm still scared shitless before each one,' she says, 'but I'm not as scared as I was.' The benefits outweigh her fears. 'You get incredibly close to people when you are crawling around in mud with them for close to twelve hours,' she says. 'And for the first time in my life I have been able to trust strangers with my physical being.' She used to get frightened of breaking bones because she didn't want to be in a cast again. Now she gets scared because she doesn't want another injury to disrupt her Tough Mudder season.

Ilene trains for the event as hard as her body will let her and believes the resultant strength has even made her slightly less vulnerable. Last year, for probably the first time in her life, she fell over and did not break a bone. When she asks her orthopaedist if she should do another event, he tells her 'as an orthopaedist, no. But as a human being, yes of course you should.' She sometimes wonders where her determination to take on these challenges comes from. When she does so, she remembers that as a younger woman she was fascinated by watching people running and became obsessed with how that might feel. To give herself some of the sensation she would search out hills in her wheelchair, and just let herself go: feeling completely alive for a few seconds was worth the risk.

Last June, Ilene was doing a Tough Mudder in Orlando and a

couple of her teammates hadn't managed to make it. One of her friends roped in a friend of hers, Daniel, an elite athlete who was planning to run the event alone. It took the team ten hours to do the ten-mile race. It was so muddy that Ilene's crutches kept getting stuck. Daniel was an enormous help, but halfway through he had to leave the event to drive his friend to the airport. A couple of hours later Ilene was surprised to see him coming back towards them through the mud. He had dropped his friend off and run the course backwards to help Team Ilene home.

This story comes with a happy ending, one that Ilene couldn't quite have imagined when she first wrote to Noah Galloway years ago. Ilene and Daniel became very close online Mudder friends and then they started dating and doing Mudder races and other events together. Last year she crewed for him at World's Toughest Mudder, staying up all night and helping him through; next year, after he moves to Connecticut to be with her, they plan to attempt the event together.

CHAPTER 9

The Gathering of the Tribes: Where Next for the Mudder Nation?

The future depends on what you do today.

— **Mahatma Gandhi**

In November 2016, I was standing on top of a hill in the Nevada desert, looking down on the gathered tribes of the Tough Mudder Nation. Fifteen hundred people were about to roar up this hill towards me to embark on the most gruelling event in our calendar, the sixth annual twenty-four-hour World's Toughest Mudder. It is, I'm thinking, almost exactly seven years since I first sat in a Brooklyn warehouse imagining this company. This was undoubtedly one of the more spectacular places that idea had journeyed to.

The hill is near the shore of Lake Las Vegas, in the foothills of the Black Mountains, not far from the giant Hoover Dam. The land here has a Mad Max appearance, like some raw red apocalyptic moonscape. It also carries with it some ghosts. For two thousand years this lake was an oasis for the nomadic Paiute tribe of Native Americans who set up camp on its shores. The tribe wore red paint to protect their skin from the desert sun, and they developed rites of passage that included body piercings and tattoos and trials of skill and endurance to strengthen health and community. Those rituals were mostly lost from this land in the last century; today Lake Las Vegas is a desert resort. Fantasy waterfront mansions and hotels crowd the shore in lush, irrigated gardens. But this afternoon, squinting in the midday sun, you could convince yourself that for one weekend, at least an echo of those ancient rituals had survived.

The World's Toughest Mudder is a special date in our calendar. We introduced the event a year after the first Tough Mudder to cater for those Mudders who wanted the ultimate obstacle challenge, something to take them beyond any other test of stamina and will. In the first couple of years the event was held at Raceway Park in New Jersey in hail and snow. Since then the daily extremes of desert temperature and frequent sandstorms in Nevada have made it an annual festival of fortitude, our own higher, faster, stronger Olympics. Every Tough Mudder weekend is about collective endeavour and shared adventure, but nowhere is the sense that 'I' has become 'we' more visible than here.

The weekend also marks the end of our year and – in introducing our new obstacles – the beginning of the year to come. It is a time for looking back on what we have achieved and looking forward to what comes next. That optimistic mind-set is crucial to negotiating a Tough Mudder course and in gearing the company to its next stages of growth. As a leader, I try to use the World's Toughest weekend to spread a message that we should always collectively enjoy and take pride in what we have created and that there is always more to create. Adventure is not a one-off experience but a state of mind.

The detail is always important. Standing on that hill waiting for the event to start, I'm excited to discover how our new obstacles, developed in the Lab, will perform. Double Rainbow, which requires some authentic Tarzan skills to swing from one trapeze bar to another; the claustrophobic upward pipe of Augustus Gloop ('like climbing up a mineshaft under a waterfall'); and, silhouetted behind me in the hill against the bright blue sky, the towering netted A-Frame that Mudders will clamber over in every five-mile lap, which we are calling, with due reverence, The Giant Wedgie.

I'm also looking forward to seeing how a few of our other innovations will go down. World's Toughest is a race as well as a challenge (though it still can only be completed in collaboration with other Mudders). Despite the fact that it requires superhuman endurance, there is a range of ages and fitness levels among the fifteen hundred starters: some are aiming for a marathon of twenty-five miles; the leading racers (about 10 per cent of the field), meanwhile, will endeavour to cover a barely credible hundred miles overnight. Those hundred miles involve thirty-five-foot cliff jumps into icy water, all the various Mud Miles and Everests that a Mudder course offers, and innumerable hard slogs up and down these sun-scorched and then moonlit sandstone hills. The first team or individual to complete that century of miles would win themselves a hundred thousand dollars. This year we have a yellow jersey bib for the overall race leader and we have a black jersey for the most miles in darkness, the King of the Night.

For the first time the event will also be televised in full. CBS is out here in force, with multiple drone cameras hovering in the desert air to capture every desperate lunge and last-gasp leap. The show will be broadcast on Christmas Day as a finale to a series on *The Road to the World's Toughest*. In another first, down in the crowd below I can also see my old friend Alex Patterson, who is hosting the live streaming of this event for millions of Mudder followers across the world, along with Mat Bell from our London office. For reasons best known to them, Alex and Mat have donned Elvis costumes for the occasion.

In keeping with the first shout-out to the tribe all those Mudder miles ago – 'participants are encouraged to leave their traditional running attire at home; costumes, tattoos and mullets are encouraged' – many of the fifteen hundred Mudders who have gathered here for this hardest challenge are also in costume. There are Mudders in top hats and tails, Mudders in tutus and Mudders wearing bandannas of their home nations – I can see Chile and Germany and Canada and New Zealand and many more. Some have come with photos of friends and brothers and mothers pinned to them, running in tribute or memory. There are teams in matching fluorescence, a few diehards in customized fatigues and legionnaires in all shades of Mudder headband from events past. There are wild beards and shaved heads and the odd Mohawk; there are also enough tattoos and piercings and body paint to have made the ancient Paiute nation proud.

There is, for all of us at TMHQ, always something magical about the sight of these most ardent devotees of our tribe pitching camp in the desert for this long weekend. They have come from the world's four corners trailing carts packed with sleeping bags and wetsuits and head torches and a cheerful determination to keep going come what may. Most also bring with them an official pit crew of family and volunteers (those that don't are catered for through the night by our 'orphan tent' dishing out coffee, energy bars, first aid, blankets and, where necessary, the odd motivational speech). As soon as they arrive, Mudders seek out friends from previous years, catch up with familiar Facebook friends and training partners, and get ready for the hours ahead. Though only six years old, this event already seems full of fierce tradition.

Walking around the tented village before the challenge begins I can't go five yards without a bear hug and a selfie. Here are our British super volunteers Miranda and Guy Richardson who are pit-crewing for the Afghanistan veteran Mark Holloway; here is Tiffany Aab, a cancer survivor who is having her head shaved prior to the event to raise money for a children's cancer charity. Here is Joe Perry, iconic 'face paint man' of many Mudder videos, veteran of nearly a hundred Mudder events ('I call this the best twenty-four hours of the year,' he says. 'All the other hours are either preparation or recovery'). Here is the Team Rubicon tent – with all the organizational know-how of numerous tours of duty – in which sixteen veteran volunteers will take it in turns to refuel during the night (encouraged in part with a promise of home-mixed margaritas every thirty miles).

Outside, I bump into E-Rock and Coach, who will run together as perhaps the most effervescent double act in the desert this weekend (even when considering the headline stars of the Las Vegas Strip). E-Rock (aka Eric Botsford) and Coach (Kyle Railton) have been warm-up MCs and Mudder ambassadors for several years. They have done a series of fitness videos for us, and E-Rock has designed the full Mudder training programme that will be a cornerstone of our Bootcamp gyms.

This morning, Coach has a plastic rose behind his ear 'for positive energy'. He is giving out family snaps of his late friend Vernon, a four-time World's Toughest Mudder, and will, he says to me, be carrying around the course a flag that bears the words 'Waiting for the Light'. These, Coach explains, are the last words Vernon texted to his wife from the top of a mountain earlier this year: 'He was waiting for sunrise to take a photo and the poor guy slipped and fell.' Coach has brought along some of Vernon's ashes to scatter, 'just to spread a little love'. He hopes to run the fifty miles Vernon was always aiming for and never quite managed.

As I walk around there is no end of stories like this one; they come at you from all sides. Everyone has a different, highly personal reason to be here. There are captains of industry and teachers, nurses and firefighters and hipsters and bankers. One man stops me to say, 'Every year, I watched the videos of this and I was like, one day you will make it. So this year I worked two jobs and saved all my tips and I'm actually here. It is so surreal.' Another embraces me with a familiar yell: 'We're living the dream, Will Dean, living the dream!'

At the starting line our MC Sean Corvelle is warming up for his longest night. He makes it a point to keep going all twenty-four hours, embracing each Mudder on every completed five-mile lap of the course – along with his sparring partner and fellow hype man, Clinton Jackson. Sean is a big-hearted man, peerless communicator of Mudder truth and mythology. In the last year, he has ministered at three Mudder weddings, using vows that are a variation of the Tough Mudder pledge.

Sean gives me a hug and greets me with something I said to him when I became a father for the first time (my daughter, Isobel, was born at the end of 2015) – a comment to the effect that I now had two babies to look after – Isobel and the Tough Mudder tribe. It makes Sean doubly proud, he says, to be a part of that latter commitment.

I remember making that comment to Sean. As any new parent will tell you, those first months bring a lot of intense emotions to the surface. When I first had those feelings as a dad I couldn't help being struck by the similarities between that sense of responsibility I felt towards my baby daughter and that I had felt in creating and nurturing Tough Mudder from inception to something like maturity.

Sean's comment out in the desert, and the surrounding Mudder nation, reminded me again of those feelings.

Some of them were about sleepless nights. Creating a company, just like bringing a child into the world, is not conducive to untroubled eight-hour rest. I feel I have dreamed about Tough Mudder every night of the last seven years. Certainly, I have rarely gone to bed not thinking about some of that day's pressing concerns, or woken up with a new set of challenges in my head. Being a founder as opposed to just being a CEO of a company creates special complications. You have a different level of emotional engagement with what you have made. I think this emotional attachment has been both a strength and a potential source of weakness for me with Tough Mudder. It has given me an inbuilt instinct to always try to keep the company true to our original values, but has at times made it harder to hand over some of that responsibility to others for whom it is sometimes just a job.

I try to use that emotional connection to keep the story of the company's journey alive for new recruits at TMHQ and to reinforce it with our more experienced staff. Telling stories to ourselves about ourselves is vital for strengthening the culture. It also reminds us just how far we have come. There is a good reason that new parents take all those photos and videos of their baby – every day a new milestone is passed, and there is an obvious desire to keep a record of each of them. When Isobel was born, I recognized a shadow of that feeling from the early days of the company. If you are putting your heart and soul into it – and Tough Mudder never gave any of us any other option – then everything about a start-up seems so vivid, and moves so fast, that you want to capture it before the next week's reality takes over and the previous week's startling new thing is forgotten. The record keeping also serves another purpose: when times are a bit tough, it reminds you what you have gone through already to get here, and it keeps you going forward.

There are ways that we have tried to keep track of that progress in the office. On the wall of Tough Mudder HQ in Brooklyn, for example, we keep a scrapbook timeline that reminds us of how far we have travelled and of some of the more challenging obstacles that we have overcome. At the beginning of that timeline there is a photograph of the first Tough Mudder starting line in Allentown, Pennsylvania, in May 2010, with those very first five hundred Mudders waiting to set off. Next to it is a picture of what then constituted the entire Tough Mudder staff celebrating the end of that first event: me and co-founder, Guy, and three interns, looking exhausted and relieved, clutching on to cold beers as if for dear life. (There is also one of me checking the depth of a snow pond on that course in the traditional way – neck deep – by wading through it.) At the far end of the timeline, up to nearly the present, is a picture of the current Tough Mudder team on our last annual retreat – 150 full-time employees, spread across four main offices, with satellites from the HQ in London and Melbourne.

That progression is measured, too, in the press clippings we have kept. An early event was marked by the *Wall Street Journal*, with the headline 'Office Workers Run Amok', and after that it quickly became something of a media rite of passage for magazines to turn their favourite (or perhaps least favourite) reporters into Tough Mudders. 'My balls still aren't speaking to me,' began one memorable

Maxim article of this kind in 2012. The August *New Yorker* made much the same general point a couple of years later, though with reference to the initiation ceremonies of the Brazilian Sateré-Mawé tribe and quotations from poet Robert Bly's cerebral bestseller *Iron John*. For this World's Toughest in Nevada there are as ever one or two journalists coming to give it a go, including a young woman from the *Daily Mail*, who has borrowed some gear, and confesses cheerfully to never having even heard of Tough Mudder before she arrived. (I resisted the urge to suggest that I hoped she didn't pray it had stayed that way at three o'clock in the morning, and instead wished her the very best of British luck.)

These reports caught something of a flavour of the progression of the company, but again, as with fatherhood, the things that I actually kept in mind were often quite random tiny moments out of the rush of daily events. Little exchanges that suddenly made all the effort worthwhile. One or two come to mind as I wander in the tented village in Nevada. Talking to the Team Rubicon guys, I'm reminded, for example, of how I once picked up the phone to a young man, aged nineteen, who called me up from Walter Reed, the big veterans' hospital in Bethesda, Maryland, just outside Washington, DC. He insisted on calling me sir. He said, 'Sir, I am signed up to do your challenge and looking forward to it, but I am calling to ask, sir, if I can have a special dispensation to go around the mud pits.'

I told him sure, of course, but did he mind me asking why?

He replied 'Sir, I'm a double amputee, so I can't go in there with my blades.' He sounded choked up to have to call me and ashamed to have to ask. He apologized for taking up my time. People always say you can't cheat a marathon but that presupposes everyone starts from the same place. In life, that is never the case. If someone doesn't feel able to do the mud pit at Tough Mudder for whatever reason, it is never a big deal.

Alongside such emotional memories, World's Toughest brings home the global spread of our tribe, and a sense, year by year, of how it continues to migrate. One of the extraordinary things about watching a company take on a life of its own is the way that its values come to express themselves in unexpected places and in unexpected languages. It must be a bit like seeing your child go off travelling for the first time and Skyping home from the jungle. I've become fascinated by the way in which national culture defines different behaviours. It is always quite amusing, for example, to see what our employees in different countries choose to highlight to me when I arrive for a briefing. These are cultural stereotypes, of course, but in my experience they almost invariably hold true. With the Americans it is always: 'This is the thing that is crushing it, Will, the thing we are selling lots of that is going to most help the P&L.' In Britain, conversely, you can bet it will be this new very clever innovation they are doing that no one else has yet thought of. In Germany they will always want to tell me about the regular process that they have most improved; with Australians, meanwhile, it will be: 'I know the business is important, Will, but you'll love this fun promo we did last week.'

In the months before November 2017 and Nevada that 'think globally, act locally' perception had taken on a new dimension for me. Before arriving in Las Vegas, I had spent a couple of weeks at the two sites of our most recent expansion: in Dubai and Shanghai. The experiences had in different ways brought home just how far we had come in our efforts to 'grow Tough Mudder as a global nation'.

In Dubai – where I hadn't been since Foreign Office days, on very different kinds of missions – I had planted a flag at the course site in the teeth of a dust storm, and then examined the various mud samples that contractors had thoughtfully brought with them to create the full Mudder experience in the desert. Seven years ago, I'd had to beg local sponsors to give us a few kegs of free beer. Now we had a global telecom company building an entire village for us just for the naming rights, and we were having involved meetings to discuss the logistics of pausing the event to enable midday prayers. We weren't in Allentown now.

If anything, in China, this realization had been even more stark. We were due to stage the first Mudder event in Shanghai, the culmination of a year of meetings and formalities. Each meeting began with translated pleasantries about how (alarmingly) young I looked, greetings that appeared to mask a degree of nervous concern about my two-day stubble and jeans and untucked shirt. There would often be twenty people in the room, seated in a semicircle: nineteen representatives from state and cultural and commercial departments on the one side, and me on the other. Never in the field of human commerce has one man given and received quite so many business cards.

My initial challenge in the Shanghai meetings lay in persuading the supremely polite and efficient Chinese officials of the reasons why anyone in their right mind would want to crawl through mud or jump into an ice bath. It was like being faced with a room full of sceptical Harvard professors all over again, with the added joy of simultaneous translation. The younger people I met seemed to get the idea of Tough Mudder, but to anyone in the room over forty, fitness and well-being were ideas confined to spa and luxury, and even then a minority interest. As part of my pitch I had a killer statistic, however.

In the United States people spend ten times on wellness what they spend on cars. In China that number is exactly reversed. Surely, I suggested, the gap had to close.

Once our Chinese partners were persuaded, they had done everything in their power to make sure the event would be a success. Tickets had sold well. The Tough Mudder site was on a former golf course on the fringes of the city – not quite Whistler Mountain, but it more than did the job. The local government had constructed brand-new roads to it just for our event. By the time I had arrived for what was planned as a grand opening ceremony, no detail had been left to chance. The site was draped in Tough Mudder logos and slogans in Mandarin; the obstacles had been constructed exactly to order. Two days before the event was due to start our course site looked invitingly ready. A day later, however, fate intervened. A typhoon ripped through that part of the city overnight and took all our obstacles and tents and banners with it, leaving the entire course under two feet of water. I stood there with my Chinese colleagues and looked across this Tough Mudder lake in disbelief.

I have learned that there are many times when you battle on regardless, and there are a few times when you must reluctantly admit defeat. Surveying the wreckage of the course we'd had to make the decision to abandon that inaugural Chinese event, with a promise to the new tribe of Shanghainese Mudders who had signed up that we would be back very soon – when it was a little less muddy. It was only the second event we'd ever had to cancel.

By the time I had arrived in Nevada for World's Toughest, the freakish storm felt like some fevered nightmare. The typhoon had left a large e-mail trail as well as a significant clean-up operation, however, so three or four hours after the Mudders had set off into the desert sun, I headed back to my hotel room to resurrect our Chinese expansion and to catch up on other business.

My in-box was swamped not only by the weather in China, but also by the latest updates on our other imminent arrival: our Bootcamp gym business. If there is a single clue to what Tough Mudder is going to look like as a grown-up company – 'show me the child at seven' – the gym initiative is central to it. One of the things we have learned and taken to heart is that the farther our event travels, the more important our model of increasing the ways for the tribe to interact with us and with each other becomes. For our Tough Mudder values and stories to circulate effectively, we need to continue to build a vibrant web of ways to share those values and stories. As Tough Mudder grows, we envisage it becoming an ecosystem of mutually supporting businesses that will help to establish ever more of those links, both through digital platforms and physical spaces.

Though its audience couldn't be much more different from Tough Mudder's, a company like Zumba, which in a decade, using a range of channels – DVDs, an instructor network, a spectrum of delivery formats – grew from a single dance fitness class to a global business, in which fifteen million people in 186 countries took weekly instruction, shows how far a good viral idea can go. Our ambition at Tough Mudder is to combine that kind of reach with the depth of emotional connection felt, as I outlined earlier, by a movement like the chapters of Harley-Davidson riders. To begin to provide not only some real sense of ownership and belonging of Tough Mudder as a lifestyle, but also the coordinates of a shareable identity – one that cuts across international boundaries and divisions of gender, race, age and income. This growth is by its nature organic. It depends on Mudders reaching out and responding to Mudders. But it is up to our business to provide the architecture for those connections and to nurture them in innovative ways.

As CEO I believe it is my responsibility to always be alive to where the new progressive energy is in the business. The Bootcamp, along with the expansion into new territories and the collaborations with CBS, is that energy now. New projects revitalize every other part of the organization and keep your own motivation high and positive. The gyms will be a key element in strengthening our tribal values and connections – a way for the tribes to gather not only annually but several times a week. To this end, we've been looking hard at the detail of how our Bootcamps can be designed to promote connection and community rather than solitary fitness goals. These details are both symbolic and practical. The gyms will, for example, not have any mirrors in the workout room – the idea is to look not at yourself but at each other. To encourage connection, the high-intensity interval training will involve circuits with a partner assigned at random – in sessions led by E-Rock on video and customized by Tough Mudder–certified coaches in person. These sessions, like the obstacles on a Tough Mudder course, will provide the framework of the Mudder experience. The real life of it – as in the Nevada desert – will develop in the connections between each gym's mini tribe.

The gym project returns me to the prove-your-hunch risk of start-up. Businesses don't come with a defined DNA for development. That energy has to be fuelled by looking forward, being prepared to keep trying new things in the context of what we have already achieved, to keep on adventuring, and never get stuck in the mud.

As I type my response to the e-mails in my hotel room, I keep one eye on the live stream feed from the desert up the road. It is, as ever, intensely gratifying and quite humbling to see all this extraordinary effort expended in the name of the movement we have built. The live stream itself is almost surreally absorbing. Alex and Mat have added head torches to their Elvis costumes but are still going strong. At midnight, I watch the first Mudders Geronimo-jump off the Cliff into the cold black water thirty-five feet below, under a big full moon. (I had tested the jump myself the Friday before the event – you are not only falling for a very, very long time but also under the water for a second or two more than you might imagine; surfacing is an extremely good feeling.) Among our teams this year is Team Blind Pete, whose members are, as their name suggests, being led by Blind Pete around the course through the night. Alex and Mat catch Pete as he emerges from the water to ask for his verdict on the Cliff and they get a Mudder response that makes me smile. Pete felt especially fortunate to be able to jump off into the darkness, he says, 'because being blind only adds to the excitement!'

For a while, Jerome Hiquet has been urging me to read *Tribe*, a book by Sebastian Junger, author of *The Perfect Storm*. It makes the case for learning from older Native American communities, and from the camaraderie of soldiers on tours of duty, to heal some of the fractures in our own societies. I have a copy at my bedside and at two or three in the morning before I drop off I start to read. As soon as I pick the book up I can see why Jerome thought it relevant to what we do. I even underline a few passages: 'Humans don't mind hardship,' Junger writes, 'in fact they thrive on it; what they mind is not feeling necessary. Modern society has perfected the art of making people not feel necessary.' Ditto to that. And another, 'In effect, humans have dragged a body with a long hominid history into an overfed, malnourished, sedentary, sunlight-deficient, sleep-deprived, competitive, inequitable and socially isolating environment with dire consequences.' I put an exclamation mark beside that one. And finally, a solution to some of these problems: 'If you want to make a society work, then you don't keep underscoring the places where you're different – you underscore your shared humanity.' I love the optimism in that idea. It might be a slogan for the Tough Mudder business we are trying to build. I go to sleep half thinking of Mudders who are taking their leaps of faith into the cold dark water below.

One of the things that the World's Toughest Mudder brings home is just how many hours there are in a single day. The longer I am away from the World's Toughest site – eating breakfast, taking a shower – it becomes harder to imagine that the event can possibly still be in progress, though the live stream tells me otherwise. At eight the following morning, twenty hours after the event began, I head back up to witness the now traditional Mudders' shared joy at the rising sun after the long hard miles of the night. Competitors are now limping a little stiffly, a few have called it a day, but most are still ploughing on. The unseasonably warm overnight conditions have allowed more people than normal to keep going without pause, so everyone is getting close to their personal distance goals. By nine in the morning, with three hours still to go, many Mudders are collecting their vests that mark fifty completed miles, a few have already clocked seventy-five miles.

The race leaders are a team of two: Ryan Atkins, already a two-time individual winner of this event, and Jon Albon from Britain. The first time Ryan came to World's Toughest in 2013 he was associated with a team from Joe De Sena's rival Spartan Race, who had signed up to prove a competitive point. That Spartan tactic backfired a little, though, as Ryan enjoyed the Tough Mudder obstacles and atmosphere so much he became a convert, and he is now one of our own ambassadors. As I walk through the course in the morning, I happen to see him and Jon scaling Everest. Despite the fact that they are leading the race – and in the knowledge that if they are first to complete a hundred miles, they will collect a special prize of a hundred thousand dollars – they still pause for a minute or two at the top of the obstacle to help a few other less athletic Mudders up and over before heading off again into the cool morning air. They have no idea I am watching. But they know that the culture demands it.

The very last hours of a World's Toughest Mudder routinely reveal some of the more extreme faces of human endeavour. Wetsuited men and women emerge from the water and mud like primeval beings striking out at land for the first time. A few – Coach and E-Rock included – still look about as fresh as they did twenty hours and fifty miles ago.

The women's race is wider open this year than in the past because the two great Mudder champions have been unable to run: Deanna Blegg is in Australia, still battling with cancer but with the promise that in 2017, 'all going well I'll be there'. Amelia Boone is nursing a back injury, though she is on-site helping Alex and Mat with the live feed. In their absence from the race the women's challenge is being led by a competitor whose name I don't recognize – Stefanie Bishop – although when I see her come through the pit lane to begin her final lap at eighty miles, I can't help thinking that she looks extremely familiar. Alex Patterson says the same.

An hour or so later at the finishing line – which Stefanie crosses turning cartwheels after eighty miles – as I am handing out congratulations and headbands and medals, that mystery is solved. Stefanie had, she confesses, run in the very first Tough Mudder in Bear Creek, but because of work and a few injury issues had not come back until this year. I realize as we talk that the reason Alex and I recognized Stefanie was that every morning for a year or so we had shared an office with her. In the corner of the original DUMBO warehouse headquarters we'd had a poster up above our desks from Bear Creek – and since Stefanie and her sister were among the few women who had taken part, the poster featured them, with the aim of encouraging more to follow. It was the memory of just how much she enjoyed that first weekend that had brought Stefanie out here seven years later to Nevada. Next year she was hoping to form a team with Amelia Boone and run a hundred miles.

At the finishing line, at high noon, Sean and Clinton are still greeting every Mudder, handing out headbands and vests, keeping up their twenty-four-hour non-stop dialogue with the tribe. Sean has probably done more hugging in one night than most people manage in a lifetime. His voice remains as deeply welcoming as ever, and as the event draws to a close, he runs through all his trademark lines one last time. 'Come on!' he yells, 'there's nothing better than your best – but your best will always make you better!' And then, on demand, his signature phrase is delivered at full volume to the returning Mudder nation: 'Tell me folks: when was the last time you did something for the first time?'

I must have heard that line from Sean a thousand times but it remains a very good question. It is by taking on and seeking out new challenges that we grow. Our brains and bodies don't thrive on standing still or backing off; they are primed for novelty and challenge. Every time we are confronted with a surprise event or a new experience, a shot of dopamine is released in the brain, making our blood pump a little faster, and firing off some positive energy in our pleasure and reward centres. It's why those who see retirement as the time to be endured between work and the end don't live as long or as actively as those who use it to embrace new challenges and take up new skills. As Tough Mudder continues to expand as a business and evolve as a community, we try to ask Sean's question of ourselves continually. It has been our belief that the example of risk taking and innovation that our business represents can become a habit and a mind-set that feeds into the lives of the entire Mudder tribe. The mechanism by which it does so is time-honoured and perhaps the real purpose of adventures: the opportunity to come home and share campfire stories about them. These stories are our lifeblood. This book has, I hope, highlighted some of the best of them.

The ongoing story of Tough Mudder itself is still, I am convinced, in its very early chapters. We are working out where it will take us, and how exactly it will unfold. I believe it is the story of a business that is not so much about branding as about belonging; the story of a twenty-first-century tribe that goes beyond borders and cultures but shares a set of values and ideas about the world. It's a tribe that will continue to grow and to connect and to prosper. It is a tribe, like all the best tribes, that was born first out of the primal ooze. Out of mud.

MUDDER LEGEND: Jim Campbell

When I started Tough Mudder, I knew that if the business became successful, it would be because those values we began with had also become the authentic values of the Tough Mudder tribe. That the soul of the company would not exist in our office or in our business strategy but in the hearts and minds of all the millions of Mudders who had earned their headband. That it would have taken on a life of its own.

Of all those Mudders no one probably understands that spirit more keenly than Jim Campbell (who long ago earned the Mudder nickname 'Da Goat'). Stories seem to follow Jim around. It's fitting that the last word in this book, this story of our first seven years and its legends, comes not from me but from him.

Jim was awarded a specially forged iron headband last September for becoming the first Tough Mudder to complete a century of events. His signature blue shirt, hydration pack and beanie hat (adorned with his native Colorado state flag) have been around since Tough Mudder's first days. He's completed six events in Canada, four in Ireland, four in Scotland, four in England and two in Germany. Aged fifty-two, he's also one of only a handful of people who have competed in all six World's Toughest Mudder events. In Las Vegas this year he again cemented his legendary status after an angry rattlesnake stopped Mudders in their tracks as they approached Everest.

Jim stepped forward with a crooked stick, trapped the snake by its neck, dispatched it briskly, and headed on his way.

'I've seen snow and sleet and hail,' he says. 'I did an event the first year in Austin, Texas, when a flash flood came when we were halfway around and washed the course away. I have got stories of the yin and yang.' Still, to date, he says, the 2011 event at Bear Creek, Colorado, was the hardest thing he has ever done. 'You went up to eleven thousand feet and had to jump in a pond covered in ice. That was proper hardcore.'

What Jim neglects to mention when he tells this story was that Bear Creek was also the first he had done after he had risen from a hospital bed and walked. A motorcycle crash in 2009 left him with his neck broken in two places and numerous other life-changing injuries. He spent six months immobile in a cerebral halo. He was told that if he was ever able to walk again it would be with a walker, if he was lucky. He had been an athlete all his life (formerly a top-ranked American Motorcyclist Association racer and a 1984 USA Olympic windsurfing team qualifier), and he refused to go gentle into that good night.

After his accident, Jim heard himself pronounced dead three times. At the crash site, they didn't take the motorcycle off him because they thought there was no point. He landed on his neck, and then the eight-hundred-pound Harley-Davidson had landed on top of him and pounded his head into the ground. He heard a paramedic tell the police, 'He'll never make it to the hospital,' as they closed the ambulance door on him. In the hospital, he 'literally and figuratively' sat up in bed and said, 'I am not going to fucking die.' He still gets emotional when he tells that story.

In all the long months of recovery, Jim, who runs his own

construction company, refused to let his future be limited by low expectations. When he first saw the ad for Tough Mudder on his Facebook page, not long after he had been allowed to move his head for the first time in six months, it felt to him a lot like a calling. And not just to him. 'There are a lot of people that have always been living this life,' he says, 'climbing through mountains on weekends and jumping in rivers and just being prepared to take on life in general. Tough Mudder found us all and made an event for us. How smart was that?'

When people ask Jim why he has done a hundred Mudders, and why he has remained so committed to the cause, he says it is not about the headbands, it is not about the beer, it is not even about the obstacles (though he enjoys all three). He says it's because you get addicted to sharing the spirit with new people. Recently he was at the event in Dallas and he shared his story with a guy who had himself been in a car accident. Jim could see in the man's eyes the place he was at because it was also the place Jim had been. He was worried he couldn't get around. Jim said, 'Even if you can't do it there are people here who will make sure you can.' And so it was proved. 'If you can come to an event on a weekend and join up with ten thousand people who think there are no problems, only challenges,' Jim says, 'why would you not keep coming back?'

I have talked in this book about the way the Tough Mudder tribe keeps the business honest, keeps the spirit of the pledge alive. Jim has made himself the embodiment of that determination. He takes responsibility not only for helping people understand the ethos of the event but also for holding us to account when things aren't up to his Tough Mudder standards. 'I don't think Will and Guy had any idea what they set in motion when they started this,' he likes to say.

'This thing grows from within. Over the years Tough Mudder has done some stuff that didn't go right, but it would be hard to ever kill this spirit, because there is such a grassroots feeling in it now of people who believe in each other and who believe in the event.'

Jim spreads that message where he can. Over the years, he has been a church-going man; now Tough Mudder occupies at least part of that space for him. 'You can argue what religion is,' he says. 'I'm a spiritual person. I've gone to church a lot in my life, and you come away saying, you know, "See you next week", and that's nice. When I do a Tough Mudder on a Sunday it is a very different experience. Nothing is being promised for the future. It's this thing that your body is doing now. The reward is right there that day. And then when you leave, you leave with a yearning for it.'

The Colorado event has a special meaning for Jim. It's his home state and the place where he learned that he could still have the life he kept hearing he had lost. He will, he says, always come back to that event no matter what.

And what does he think of the idea that he embodies the Tough Mudder spirit, keeps the flame?

'It's an honour more than a responsibility,' he says. 'I know this all grew out of a business plan and all of that. But for many thousands of people it has become something much more than a business. I am just one pebble on the beach of Tough Mudder. It is going to keep finding special people and drawing them in. And you know what the great thing about that is? I get to keep meeting those people.' Jim laughs at the prospect of the expanding tribe. 'The thing is,' he says, 'Tough Mudders never stop.'

Acknowledgements

Before I founded the company, I simply had no idea what a long and, at times, draining process building an organization could be – let alone a company as logistically complex and emotionally engaging as Tough Mudder. I could not have done it without the love and support of my close friends and family. There is a line in the film *The Descendants* where George Clooney explains, 'You give your children enough money to do something but not enough to do nothing.' My parents sacrificed a great deal to give my sister and me all that is really important in life. Alongside my ever-patient, loving and understanding sister, Liz, my parents have stood by me in all I have done despite their periodic deep reservations. I am fortunate to have a handful of true friends. Many have known me since I was a shy, lost little boy a long way from home. Knowing I have loyal friends who will always be there for me – regardless of my many failings – has got me through some very tough and lonely times. Thank you to every one of you. You know who you are. My wife, Katie Palms, is my absolute rock. She is all the things I am not and I would not be half the man I am today without her warmth, kindness, perceptive wisdom and sense of humour. I may not have taken much away from my two years at

Acknowledgements

Harvard, but had I not met Katie when I did, I shudder to think where I might be today. She believed in me when almost no one else did and I am very grateful for all of her love and support. She is a truly exceptional woman.

I want to thank my co-founder, Guy Livingstone. Those early years were very tough but Guy's stoicism, work ethic and support got us through. Without him, I am not sure there would be a Tough Mudder Incorporated today. I am also hugely appreciative of all the early joiners at TMHQ, particularly Alex Patterson, Sheetal Aiyer, Paul Simcox, Jesse Bull, Nolan Kombol and Kelley Kantarian. You joined me when the world was still asking us how we planned to spell 'Mudder'. I hope I have been able to repay the enormous faith you placed in me. Similarly, I am grateful to my Harvard business plan competition teammates Sean Eldridge and Ben Mayson. I will always remember those carefree evenings brainstorming potential business names in the bars of Cambridge, Massachusetts.

Many thanks to my executive team of Adam Slutsky, Don Baxter, Jerome Hiquet, Donna Goldsmith and Marc Ackerman as well as the Bootcamp team of Cathrin Bowtell, David Spindler and Eric Botsford for making time to be interviewed. Sean Corvelle, Clinton Jackson, Kyle Railton (Coach) and Gil Kolirin deserve special credit for their brilliant and unique insights into the Mudder tribe. Other interviewees I would like to thank include Matt Siben, Joe De Sena, Duane Policelli, Jenn Hyman, Sarah Robb O'Hagan, Jake Wood and Jon Brown. I hope you are able to see the colour and humour you contributed to the book. I am also grateful to everyone at TMHQ who has supported me through this project despite having so many other priorities to juggle, particularly Angela Alfano, Jodi Kovacs, Anthony Key, Bobby Donovan and Rob Zimmerman. Special thanks to my friend Dmitry Gudkov for supplying so many of the images from our events over the years.

I am deeply indebted to all the Mudder Legends for taking the time to tell your stories so bravely and with such patience and dignity. I hope we did you justice. James Brown, Louise Clifford, Aidan Harrison, Will Cattermole, Chelsea Campbell, Joe Perry, Amelia Boone, Stef Bishop, Mark Holloway, Ken Jacobus, Erik Jenkins, Melissa Dugan, and Miranda and Guy Richardson also deserve special credit. You embody the very best of the Tough Mudder tribe and are a credit to the community.

Thanks to everyone who gave me the confidence to write a book in the first place, particularly Philip Delves Broughton, Eric Ries, Adam Grant, Brad Feld, Dave Kidder, Rachel Botsman, Mark Smith and Strauss Zelnick. I am exceptionally grateful for the faith shown in me by agent Toby Mundy and the entire team at Penguin Books. Special thanks to Joel Rickett, Stephanie Frerich, David Over, Merry Sun, Natalie Horbachevsky, Adrian Zackheim, Will Weisser and Tara Gilbride. You have all been a joy to work with and have taught me much.

Most important, I want to thank my co-writer, Tim Adams. While this may be my story, Tim deserves all the credit for bringing it to life and capturing my voice so perfectly. Unassuming, perceptive, witty and unfailingly patient, I could not have hoped for a better partner. I hope we get to work together again one day. There is no way I could have done it without him.

Finally, thank you to everyone who has ever worked at TMHQ, every volunteer who has ever helped out at one of our events, and every one of the three-million-plus participants at our events. It takes a tribe. We are not curing cancer but I like to think in some small way we are making a positive difference in the world.

Index

Index

Index

'The power of internal motivation, great leadership and team building. Will Dean demonstrates all this and more in *It Takes a Tribe*'

BRANDON WEBB, former Navy SEAL, author of *The Red Circle* and *Total Focus*, and CEO of Hurricane Group

'This book shows that an entrepreneur with imagination and nerve can make a real difference by creating life-changing opportunities for thousands of people across the world'

GENERAL SIR NICK PARKER, former commander-in-chief of the British Army

'Will Dean has created one of the most original and inventive brands in the world, and his story will be valuable for anyone looking to change the rules of business'

BRETT YORMARK, CEO of the Brooklyn Nets